# Training Games for the Learning Organization

# Training Games for the Learning Organization

**James J. Kirk**
Western Carolina University

**Lynne D. Kirk**

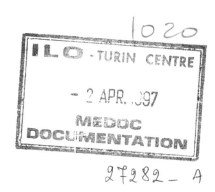
**McGraw-Hill**

New York   San Francisco   Washington, D.C.   Auckland   Bogotá
Caracas   Lisbon   London   Madrid   Mexico City   Milan
Montreal   New Delhi   San Juan   Singapore
Sydney   Tokyo   Toronto

Library of Congress Catalog Card Number: 96-78073

# McGraw-Hill

### A Division of The McGraw-Hill Companies

1 2 3 4 5 6 7 8 9 0   EDW/EDW   9 0 1 0 9 8 7 6 (PBK)
1 2 3 4 5 6 7 8 9 0   EDW/EDW   9 0 1 0 9 8 7 6 (LL)


ISBN 0-07-034924-X (PBK)
ISBN 0-07-034923-1 (LL)



*The sponsoring editor for this book was Richard Narramore, the editing supervisor was Penny Linskey, and the production supervisor was Pamela Pelton. It was set in Bookman by James J. Kirk.*

**Drawings by Mathew J. Kirk and Brandon A. Kirk.**

*Printed and bound by Edwards Brothers.*

McGraw-Hill books are available at special quantity discounts to use as premiums and sales promotions, or for use in corporate training programs. For more information, please write to the Director of Special Sales, McGraw-Hill, 11 West 19th Street, New York, NY 10011. Or contact your local bookstore.

This book is printed on acid-free paper.

# CONTENTS

## 3. Meta Learning: Games for learning how to learn

## 4. Remodeling: Games for exposing and changing the ways we see the world

## 5. Group Portraits: Games for involving everyone in the organization's vision

## 6. Hybrid Learning: Games that facilitate group learning

## 7. Parts and Engines: Games for focusing on the intra-workings of an organization's parts

# The Gaming Table

| Concept | Game | Page |
|---------|------|------|

# Preface

If you have been looking for fun, innovative, concrete ways to make your company a learning organization, you have picked up the right resource. *Training Games for the Learning Organization* contains 50 exciting games to help employees put aside old ways of thinking, to become more open with one another, and to better grasp how their company really operates. By playing games like Five Star Goals, players will discover new ways of fashioning a company vision that co-workers get excited about, and learn how to better work together to achieve shared goals. As a collection, the games hold powerful ideas successfully used by companies that have decided to take charge of their own destinies.

*James J. Kirk*
*Lynne D. Kirk*

# Training Games for the Learning Organization

# Chapter One

# Introduction

The term "learning organization" was first used in the 1980s by Richard Pascal. However, it was the publication of Peter Senge's best seller, *The Fifth Discipline*, in 1990 that popularized the phrase. Because this commonly used expression means different things to different people, the authors offer their definition of the term before proceeding any further. As used in this book, *learning organization* refers to "any company having a climate that speeds up individual and group learning."

While thousands of individuals have purchased *The Fifth Discipline*, many buyers confess that they have never actually read the book in its entirety. Many of those who have read the book admit to having difficulties in understanding and applying its ideas. It is in this context that *Training Games for the Learning Organization* is offered as a resource to assist trainers, group facilitators, organization developers, adult educators, team leaders, supervisors, and managers in comprehending and putting to use a variety of learning organization concepts. It is recommended that *Training Games for the Learning Organization* be used in conjunction with *The Fifth Discipline* and other works on the learning organization. For this reason, most of the games in this volume are grouped according to Senge's "five disciplines," which include systems thinking (comprehending the big picture), personal mastery (doing the job well), mental models (critically questioning old assumptions), shared vision (arriving at a collective purpose), and team learning (working together collaboratively). The other games in the book focus on learning how to be a better learner.

## Freedom to Learn Games

It is the basic human need to learn, grow, and achieve personal mastery that fuels and provides substance to all learning organizations. Thus, no organization can truly be a learning organization without its individual members being free to learn. Employees must be taught, encouraged, and granted permission to become creative architects of their own work lives. Furthermore, they must not allow themselves to think of personal mastery as some elevated state of super human perfection. Rather, employees must permit themselves to think of personal mastery as a process of continuous growth and development.

The games in Chapter Two are designed to foster personal mastery within work groups and throughout an organization. In the game *Climatize* players learn which conditions encourage employees to engage in personal mastery. The games *Please Pass the Risketts* and *Risk Style Decoder* address limits to individual mastery. The game *Please Pass the Risketts* focuses on limits imposed by the employing organizations, whereas *Risk Style Decoder* explores limits individuals sometimes place on themselves. *Learning Your C, C, C's* and *Motivation Bingo* address the matter of motivating workers to engage in personal mastery. *Learning Your C, C, C's* considers reasons why people might voluntarily engage in new learning, and *Motivation Bingo* identifies five factors that make employees want to work harder. The games *Forcecasting Follies* and *RunOn Rewards* concern themselves with keeping personal mastery alive. *Forcecasting Follies* looks at forces that are capable of supporting or hindering personal mastery. *RunOn Rewards* stimulates thinking on potential ways of rewarding or encouraging workers to engage in personal mastery. Finally, Smart *Acts* provides participants examples of actual companies who are well on their way to establishing supportive learning climates.

## Meta Learning Games

Not everyone agrees on what constitutes learning. Many workers consider learning simply "the act of acquiring new information." For some, learning means "picking up new behaviors and skills." Others look on learning as "gaining new insights through personal experiences." The games in Chapter Three provide players the opportunity to engage in meta learning -- to look at learning from a variety of perspectives and to learn and practice ways of increasing their own learning capabilities.

The game *Teaching Machine* offers players four definitions of learning and how each might be applied in work situations. *Top This* and *Domain* focus on various levels and categories of learning. Knowledge gained here can help employees develop their higher-level thinking capabilities and select learning strategies appropriate to the type of learning they wish to undertake. *Study Buddies* exposes players to different learning styles. Participants learn about their personal learning preferences as well as those of coworkers. *Action Figures* and *Do It Myself* explore two approaches to learning highly favored by many employees, experiential learning and self-directed learning. *Remember This* helps players improve their memory. The game *Power Learners Play-Offs* highlights the personality traits of effective "learner leaders." Learner leaders have been successfully used in some organizations to facilitate rapid, widespread strategic learning.

## Remodeling Games

Mental models are images, assumptions, and beliefs that everyone carries around in their heads. They include strongly held beliefs about self, family members, employing organizations, and the world at large which exist in the subconscious. These mental maps help people simplify, organize, and make sense of their complex world. A distinguishing characteristic of learning organizations is that they operate from a strong factual base. Learning organizations are willing to continuously discard or revise obsolete and sometimes treasured beliefs and embrace new and unfamiliar mental models.

The games in Chapter Four are intended to serve two primary purposes: (1) to help participants gain a better understanding of the concept of mental models and (2) to get employees actively involved in testing and revising of their own mental models. The game *Bewitching Behaviors* highlights some of the rather bizarre mental models at work in American society, whereas *Gap Gapers Feud* assesses the credibility players give selected corporate models. The game *Mind Readers' Rally* underscores common discrepancies between spoken and unspoken models. *Diversity Screen* demonstrates how mental models in the form of stereotypes affect employees' behaviors. *Great Siberian Freeze-Off* illustrates the process of unfreezing, restructuring, and refreezing mental models. Two games in Chapter Four, *Who in OD Am I* and *Senge's Tiles,* test players' knowledge of organization models. *Walking the Talk* provides participants with a seven-step model for becoming a learning organization.

## Group Portraits Games

In the learning organization all workers, regardless of their position, are invited and provided with opportunities to create, test, communicate, and promote the company's mission. Employees are asked to play a strategic part in setting the goals and quality standards that will turn their company's shared vision into reality. Workers are also encouraged and given assistance in setting and aligning their own visions and goals with those of the organization. In this way learning organizations have a definite advantage over their competitors: They are able to benefit from the collective intelligence, creative know-how, and commitment of all employees.

The games in Chapter Five are aimed at helping players understand and actively participate in such strategic organization processes as collective visioning, goal setting, and the establishment of performance standards. The game *Mystery Missions* takes players to the starting point of most strategic planning -- creation of a company mission statement. Participants learn about their company's mission and compare it to those of other well-known organizations. Three games in the chapter help trainees address critical aspects of the visioning process: Vision *Telling* gives players practice in communicating a vision to others, *Vision Testing 1,2,3* shows the importance of testing potential vision statements, and *Dimesworth Buy In* draws attention to the crucial issue of selling a new vision to key stakeholders. *Bench Pinching* and *Five Star Goals* introduce players to benchmarking and criteria for effective goals. They can be used in setting goals and quality standards that when accomplished will turn the company vision into reality. *Resister Blisters* addresses the issue of resistance to change. It can be used by group members to better understand and overcome the inevitable resistance some of their planned changes will face both within and outside the team. The game *Hands Up* involves players in reflecting on their own individual missions or personal visions.

## Hybrid Learning Games

People can learn and think of more things collectively than they can individually. This is due to the fact that people learn from one another. Furthermore, the ideas expressed by one person can set in motion a sweeping avalanche of ideas. In a matter of seconds a work group is can become a thinking machine, producing a set of answers to heretofore unsolvable company problems or coming up with revolutionary new product ideas.

The games in Chapter Six are directed at promoting group learning through a favorable communication environment, enhanced individual communication skills, cooperative learning practices, and effective learning facilitation. Two games, *Domino Communico* and *Unmentionables*, help groups establish supportive communication climates in which open and candid discussions take place. In games like *Blind Reflections, Body Listening, Question My Question*, and *Sound Off* players have the opportunity to improve individual communication skills. *Blind Reflections* increases listening and reflecting skills, *Body Listening* advances body language skills, *Question My Question* enhances questioning skills, and *Sound Off* improves communications between the sexes. *Jigsaw* engages players in a cooperative learning exercise. The game *Team Leading Roles* introduces players to three group learning facilitation roles and their appropriate uses.

## Parts and Engine Games

An engine has many parts and for any engine to function at its full potential all parts must be operational. The same principle holds for organizations. Organizations are made up of interrelated elements that function as a whole (i.e., a system). Changes in one element or part of the system can cause changes in other elements. In fact, a change in one critical part (e.g., customer service) can set off a chain reaction of continuous cause-and-effect events that ripple and loop throughout an entire company. Depending upon the effect of the change, overall company performance can be either greatly enhanced or diminished.

Studying the relatedness of elements in an organization is sometimes referred to as "systems thinking." It is a practice carried on in all learning organizations. The games in Chapter Seven arm participants with selected concepts and tools they can use in their own systems thinking. *Six-Box Puzzle* and *Mind or Soul* introduce players to the concept of systems and subsystems. *Life Cycle* and *Storming Norming* help players gain an understanding of predictable changes that occur in systems and work teams over time. The three games, *Archetyping, Fishbone Puzzle*, and *Human Flow Chart* supply three graphic tools that can be used to chart and analyze cause-and-effect relationships among system elements.

## Using This Book

How Training *Games for the Learning Organization* is used will greatly depend upon the user's knowledge of the learning organization and the learning objectives that she or he hopes to achieve. Regardless of how a reader chooses to use the book, it is highly recommended that all first-time users familiarize themselves with the content and structure of the volume prior to playing any of the games. This can easily be accomplished by scanning the Table Of Contents and the Gaming Table. In browsing the

Table of Contents, the reader will see that all fifty games are grouped according to six topics (freedom to learn, meta learning, remodeling, group portraits, hybrid learning, and parts and engines). Upon examining the Gaming Table, the reader will discover an alphabetical listing of the 48 games according to their content. A more comprehensive understanding of the contents and layout of the book can be gained by carefully reading through the preceding sections of this chapter. In addition to providing a brief definition of a learning organization, the sections describe the central themes of each chapter and their related games.

Once a reader is familiar with the content and structure of the book, she or he is ready to look at the games themselves. Each game is set up in the following standard format.

## The Name of the Game

TOPIC — An overview of the theme or concept the game teaches.

LEARNING OBJECTIVE — What players should be able to do after playing the game.

NUMBER OF PARTICIPANTS — The number of players the game will accommodate. Most games can be revised by the user to accommodate more or fewer participants.

PLAYING TIME — An approximate amount of time needed to play the game.

REQUIRED MATERIALS — List of all materials needed to play the game.

TO PLAY — Specific step-by-steps instructions to follow when playing the game. A debriefing section gives activities for processing what was learned during the game.

VARIATION — Suggestions for changing how the game is played. Many of the suggestions provide ideas for customizing the content of a game for a particular company or audience.

FOR MORE INFORMATION — Source(s) where facilitators can secure additional information on the topic of the game.

Users, acquainted with the content, structure, and standard game format used in *Training Games For The Learning Organization*, will find it easy to locate games that meet their specific training needs.

# Chapter Two

# Freedom to Learn Games

# Climatize

**TOPIC**            Favorable learning climate

Companies that wish to foster and nurture active learning must establish a favorable organization climate. By establishing specific operating procedures (e.g., empowering employees to make decisions), allocating resources for particular expenditures (e.g., providing training for all workers), and rewarding employees for certain behaviors (e.g., rewarding employees for trying something new), companies can influence what employees do and learn on the job.

**LEARNING**
**OBJECTIVE**        Participants will become aware of the things their organization can do to create a more favorable learning climate.

**NUMBER OF**
**PARTICIPANTS**     Any number divided into groups of three players each

**PLAYING TIME**     10-15 minutes

**REQUIRED**
**MATERIALS**        Learning Climate Board, a set of Climate Tiles for each group, flip chart, and markers

**TO PLAY**
1. Introduce participants to the concept of a "learning climate."
2. Go over the learning objective of the game.
3. Explain to participants that they are about to play a game where they will compete with two other players in the collection of Climate Tiles. The person in each group to collect the most pairs of tiles will be considered a winner.
4. Have participants divide into groups of three players.
5. Provide each group with a Learning Climate Board and a set of 36 Climate Tiles.
6. Direct players to place the Learning Climate Board in the center of the group.
7. Have the group choose a dealer to shuffle the tiles.
8. Direct all dealers to place 18 tiles on the board faceup. The first nine tiles are placed on the board three tiles across and three rows down. The next six tiles are centered on top of the previous tiles two

tiles across and three rows down. The remaining three tiles are centered on top of the previous two layers. They are placed one tile across and three rows down in the middle of the board.

9. Once the 18 tiles have been placed on the board, ask dealers to deal the remaining 18 tiles to players in their groups. Each player should end up with six tiles

10. Advise participants that the person to the left of the dealer plays first. The object of the game is form a matching set of tiles either from uncovered tiles on the board, tiles in one's hand, or a combination of the two. Only uncovered tiles can be removed from the board. Furthermore, a tile can only be removed from the board if there is a matching uncovered tile on the board or if the player has a matching tile in her or his hand.

11. Inform players that once a match has been found they are to place the tiles faceup in front of them and continue playing. When a player is unable to lay down any matching tiles, play goes to the next player on the left. Play continues until all tiles have been removed from the board or all players can no longer play.

12. Have players continue their games until finished.

13. Have the people in each group with the most tile matches stand. Declare them winners.

14. Debrief players. Have players examine their tiles. List on a flip chart the favorable learning conditions that exist in their learning organization. Discuss how such conditions foster organization learning. Identify the conditions on the tiles that are absent from their organizations. Brainstorm ways of changing the organization climate to include some of the conditions.

**VARIATION**

Have players make up their own climate tiles and play according to the above directions. As players lay down sets of matching tiles have them tell how the condition fosters learning at their organization. Play a super game of Climatize by using two sets of tiles on a six-by-six matrix board. In addition to using the tiles provided for this game, use an additional set created by participants.

**FOR MORE INFORMATION**

Kline, P. & Saunders, B. (1993). *Ten steps to a learning organization.* Arlington, VA: Great Ocean Publishers.

## Climate Tiles

To make one set of Climate Tiles, make four photocopies of the following items on card-stock paper and cut out the cards.

| | | |
|---|---|---|
| **FREEDOM TO SPEAK** | **STRESS NOT DISTRESS** | **INNOVATION REWARDED** |
| **LEARN FROM MISTAKES** | **LEARN FROM ONE ANOTHER** | **REMAINING FLEXIBLE** |
| **SELF-DIRECTED LEARNING** | **MANAGEMENT EDUCATION** | **ALL EMPLOYEES TRAINED** |

**Learning Climate Board**

To make Learning Climate Boards, photocopy the following item on card-stock paper.

**Self-Directed Learning**

**Learning From Mistakes**

# CLIMATIZE

**Innovation Rewarded**

**Freedom To Speak**

# FORCECASTING FOLLIES

| | |
|---|---|
| **TOPIC** | Force field analysis |

As individuals strive to achieve their personal visions, they encounter numerous forces. Some forces (i.e., driving forces) support movement toward the vision. Other forces (i.e., restraining forces) block movement. The resulting condition is sometimes referred to as "creative tension." To achieve their personal visions individuals must increase the strength of the driving forces and diminish the power of the restraining forces.

| | |
|---|---|
| **LEARNING OBJECTIVE** | Participants will be able to conduct a force field analysis. |
| **NUMBER OF PARTICIPANTS** | Any number |
| **PLAYING TIME** | 12-15 minutes |
| **REQUIRED MATERIALS** | Pencils, dice, Forcecasting Worksheet, flip chart, and markers |

**TO PLAY**

1. Introduce Kurt Lewin's Force Field Analysis Model.
2. Go over the learning objective for the game.
3. Explain to players that they are going to explore some of the forces that might work in favor of a planned change and other forces that might work against such a change.
4. Inform participants that the object of the game is to correctly forecast the strength of the various supporting and opposing forces.
5. Pass out a pencil, one die, and a copy of the Forcecasting Worksheet to each player.
6. On the lines marked "Planned Change" ask players to record a personal change they would like to make or goal they would like to achieve in the coming year.
7. In the column labeled " For Change," on the three long lines below the planned change, have participants write three things that might help in making the change or achieving the goal.
8. In the column labeled "Against Change," in the three long lines above the recorded planned change,

ask players to write three things that might work against making the change or achieving the goal.

9. In the column labeled "Predicted Strength" have each player estimate on a scale from 1 to 6 the strength of each supporting and each restraining force. (6=extremely powerful force, 1=extremely weak force)

10. Once players have predicted the strength of each force, have them roll a die to determine the strength of the first opposing force. Ask them to record this number on the top line of the column labeled "actual strength."

11. Proceeding down the "Actual Strength" column, have participants repeat step 10 until the actual strength of the six forces have been recorded.

12. To compute their scores, direct players to circle all cases in which they correctly forecasted the strength of a particular supporting or opposing force. Have them give themselves one point for each correctly forecasted force.

13. Declare the player(s) with the highest score(s) winners.

14. Debrief players. Talk about some of the forces which typically work in favor of or against making a change or achieving a goal. Have players share the feelings they have when the restraining forces seem to be so much more powerful than the driving forces. On a flip chart, list some creative ways of strengthening the driving forces and weakening the restraining forces. Get players' opinions on how accurately the strength of driving and restraining forces can be predicted.

**VARIATION**

Have a volunteer from the audience present a planned change in her or his organization. Ask participants to come up with three driving and three restraining forces for that change. Get three volunteers to come forward to represent the driving forces and three more to represent the restraining forces. Direct the three persons representing the driving forces to stand to your left and the three persons representing the restraining forces to stand to your right. Pin labels on each of these players identifying the name of their particular force. Have the players record on a small sheet of paper the power (i.e., a number from 1 to 10) they believe their force would have on the stated change. Now have members of the audience predict the strengths the "force" people gave their respective forces. For each force strength the audience predicts correctly, award the audience a point. For each force strength the audience incorrectly predicts, award the group of force representatives a point. Declare the side (audience vs. force representatives) with the most points winners.

**FOR MORE INFORMATION**

Lewin, K. (1951). *Field theory in social science.* New York: Harper.
Senge, P. (1990) *The fifth discipline.* New York: Doubleday/Currency.

# FORCECASTING WORKSHEET

| Against Change | Predicted Strength | Actual Strength |
|---|---|---|
| _____ | _____ | _____ |
| _____ | _____ | _____ |
| _____ | _____ | _____ |

**Planned**

**Change**

| For Change | Predicted Strength | Actual Strength |
|---|---|---|
| _____ | _____ | _____ |
| _____ | _____ | _____ |
| _____ | _____ | _____ |

# LEARNING YOUR C, C, C s

TOPIC

Motivation to learn

Individuals choose to learn for a variety of reasons. Sometimes new learning is undertaken as a result of a personal crisis. For example, the sudden loss of one's hearing may motivate a person to learn how to read lips. On other occasions a person may be coerced into learning a new skill. For example, a librarian may have her job threatened if she doesn't learn how to operate a new computerized card catalog system. Sometimes people learn new things for the sake of camaraderie. For example, an employee learns to play golf so he can socialize with coworkers from the office. There are also instances when new learning is taken on for the sake of a challenge. For example, a violinist may choose to learn a particularly difficult piece of music. Challenge-motivated learning is often a manifestation of the basic human need to grow and develop.

LEARNING OBJECTIVE

Participants will be able to generate ways of getting employees to engage in more challenge-motivated learning activities.

NUMBER OF PARTICIPANTS

Any number divided into small groups of three to five each

PLAYING TIME

15-20 minutes

REQUIRED MATERIALS

Pencils, a deck of 32 Motivator Cards for each group, and a set of four Learning Activity Cards for each player

TO PLAY

1. Introduce participants to four learning motivators; crisis, coercion, camaraderie, and challenge.
2. Go over the learning objective of the game.
3. Pass out a pencil and a set of Learning Activity Cards to each participant.
4. Have participants write a different learning activity on each of their Learning Activity Cards. The activities should have occurred during the past 12 months.
5. On the opposite side of each card, ask players to write the underlying motivation for undertaking the

new learning (i.e., crisis, coercion, camaraderie, challenge).

6. Direct players to divide into small groups of three to five players.

7. Pass out a deck of Motivator Cards to each group of players. Request that the cards be placed facedown.

8. Explain that the game begins with the person with the shortest last name going first. These players are to draw the top card from the Motivator Cards draw pile. If they have a Learning Activity Card in their hand with the same motivator (e.g., challenge), they are to read the associated learning activity and place the two cards faceup in front of them. Play then proceeds to the person on their left. If the first player does not have a Learning Activity Card in her or his hand with a matching motivator written on it, the player is to discard the Motivator Card faceup on a discard pile. Play continues with the person to the player's left, who may either draw the top card from the draw pile or the top card from the discard pile. When the draw pile is exhausted, the discard pile should be reshuffled, placed facedown, and used as a new draw pile.

9. Inform participants that play continues around the group clockwise until a player has matched all four of her or his Learning Activity Cards. This person becomes the winner of the group.

10. Debrief players. Ask players to share which motivator (i.e., crisis, coercion, camaraderie, challenge) accounted for the majority of their new learning activities within their group. Entertain various explanations for the prevalence or infrequence of certain motivators. Ask trainees to pretend that they could control the frequency of their motivators for the next year. Have them tell which would be the most frequent and least frequent motivators. Discuss the reasons behind their answers. Brainstorm ideas for getting employees to engage in more challenge-motivated learning activities at work.

**VARIATION**     Come up with your own group of motivators for the game or have participants devise their own motivators. For example, the game could be played with two motivators--internal motivators and external motivators. Discuss ways of achieving greater balance between the number of learning activities which are internally and externally motivated.

**FOR MORE INFORMATION**    Knowles, M. (1984). *The adult learner: A neglected species* (3rd ed.). Houston: Gulf.

## Motivator Cards

To prepare a deck of Motivator Cards, make four photocopies of the following items on card-stock paper and cut out the cards.

**CRISIS**

**CRISIS**

**COERCION**

**COERCION**

**CAMARADERIE**

**CAMARADERIE**

**CHALLENGE**

**CHALLENGE**

## Learning Activity Cards

To prepare Learning Activity Cards, photocopy the following items on card-stock paper and cut them out. Prepare enough cards to provide each player four cards.

# MOTIVATION BINGO

| | |
|---|---|
| **TOPIC** | Motivating employees |

According to Herzberg's hygiene motivation theory, there are certain factors that motivate workers to work harder. They include achievement (the successful accomplishment of a task or project), recognition (official acknowledgment of a task or project well done), advancement (being promoted), responsibility (being placed in charge of important projects or functions), and the work itself (tasks and projects the employee finds personally fulfilling). Collectively, these reinforcers contribute to the ongoing process of personal mastery.

**LEARNING OBJECTIVE**

Using Herzberg's "motivators" participants will be able to come up with ways of motivating employees.

**NUMBER OF PARTICIPANTS**

Any number

**PLAYING TIME**

25-30 minutes

**REQUIRED MATERIALS**

Motivation Bingo playing boards, Master Motivation Bingo playing board, draw pieces, and board markers

**TO PLAY**

1. Review key concepts of Herzberg's motivation hygiene theory.
2. Go over the learning objective for the game.
3. Distribute playing boards and markers to all players. Inform players that the first column lists Herzberg's five motivators.
4. Explain that the game is similar to bingo, except that in Motivation Bingo, players must first identify which one of Herzberg's five motivators tends to motivate them the most. Furthermore, you win the game by being the first player to have five markers in the row (e.g., the Achievement row) which a player identified at the beginning of the game as being her or his prime motivator.
5. Have players identify which one of Herzberg's five motivators tends to motivate them the most by placing a bingo marker in that cell on their boards.

6. Begin playing by blindly selecting a draw piece containing a motivation example.

7. Read the example aloud twice.

8. Ask players to place a marker in any cell on their boards containing the example read aloud.

9. The facilitator should place the draw piece on the Master Motivation Bingo Board for future reference.

10. Remind players that they are to call out "Bingo" as soon as they get all five cells covered in their selected motivation role.

11. Repeat steps six and seven until a player calls "Bingo."

12. Have the person who called "Bingo" read her or his answers aloud while you call out the correctness of each answer. If all answers are correct, declare her or him the winner. If one of the answers is incorrect, resume play until someone wins.

13. Debrief players. Have players discuss whether the examples on their bingo board would be the kinds of things which might motivate them to worker harder. Ask them to list five examples for their major motivator (i.e., achievement, advancement, recognition, responsibility, or the work itself). Direct players to divide into different groups (e.g., departments, organizations, job categories) and rank order the five hygiene factors in terms of their power to motivate workers to engage in personal mastery. Rank one as being the most powerful and rank five as the least powerful. Compare and account for differences among the groups.

**VARIATION**

Have participants play the game using their own custom-made boards. Pass out copies of blank bingo boards. Ask participants to print their own examples in the 15 blank spaces. Play the game according to the above directions except for rolling two dice to determine which examples (spaces) participants get to cover with their markers. Numbers on the first die will determine the row on the board (i.e., 1=Achievement, 2=Advancement, 3=Recognition, 4=Responsibility, and 5=the Work Itself). The number on the second die will indicate the column on the board (i.e., 1=B, 2=I, 3=N, 4=G, and 5=O). If a six is rolled on either die, they must be rolled again. Have two players read an example aloud prior to placing a marker on any square. Debrief as you did in the original version of this game.

**FOR MORE**
**INFORMATION**       Herzberg, F., Mausner, B. & Snyderman, B. (1959). *The motivation to work.* New York: Wiley.

## Master Board

To prepare a complete master board, photocopy both master board pages on card-stock paper.

## Draw Pieces

To prepare a set of draw pieces, photocopy the master board on card-stock paper and cut out the 50 case cells.

## Playing Boards

To prepare a set of Motivation Bingo playing boards, photocopy the following game boards on card-stock paper.

# Master Board

| ACHIEVEMENT | ADVANCEMENT | RECOGNITION | RESPONSIBILITY | WORK ITSELF |
|---|---|---|---|---|
| Now that she has mastered a new filing system, Darlene can proudly find any document in seconds. | Professor Smith at Hardwork University, after writing a best-seller, advances to associate professor. | For 10 years of service, Jane gets a brass plaque | Because she has demonstrated patience, Margie now handles complaints in key accounts. | Matt thinks that spending his days creating toys is a dream job. |
| Lennie is thrilled that he has reached his sales goal this month. | Keeping her cookie line producing at maximum output, gets Maggie promoted to manager. | For outstanding sales, Al is congratulated in the company newsletter. | With her upgraded keyboard skills, Barbara is allowed to do typing for company executives. | Lydia finds creating new computer software an exciting challenge. |
| Zelda is gratified that she can now answer all technical questions about the appliances she sells. | Landing the largest new customer in five years gets Walter named account executive. | For completing the training course with high marks, Marilyn receives a framed diploma. | Because Jeff works so responsibly at the fast-food restaurant, he gets to close for the boss on weekends. | Legal assistant Marilyn finds doing research on a case of particular interest to her fulfilling. |
| Mike is pleased that he can now present ideas to his firm's top management without appearing nervous. | Darin's quality customer service at the bank has led to his advancement to head teller. | As employee of the month, Cecil's picture is in the city newspaper. | Fred manages his bottling division with such good results his supervisor allows him to do all the hiring. | Monty gets to create a company training course that he's wanted to do for five years. |
| Martha is elated that she's finished the fine details of the jewelry for the company's spring collection. | Liz's willingness to handle difficult cases results in her being appointed supervisor of child welfare. | For her superior classroom skills, Millie is named "Teacher of the Year." | Diane's proficiency in visualizing results causes her boss to assign her complex floral arrangements. | Professor Don is elated about teaching a class on his pet interest, primate socialization. |

# Master Board (Continued)

| ACHIEVEMENT | ADVANCEMENT | RECOGNITION | RESPONSIBILITY | WORK ITSELF |
|---|---|---|---|---|
| Wilma, the school custodian, is very happy she can finally control the new floor scrubber. | Ben's loyalty to his co-workers gained him his new rank of Sergeant at the Highway Patrol. | John's creative advertising art is displayed in the agency's office lobby. | Phyllis' articles on local events affords her a chance to try her hand at national news stories. | Phil enjoys making one-of-a-kind items in a custom machine shop. |
| Postmaster Ben is proud he can address 90% of his customers at the Heathville post office by name. | Always willing to help new employees learn necessary skills, Betty is elevated to technical trainer. | For her hard work in researching a cure for Alzheimer's, Mary is asked to address Congress. | Brad's grocery shelving ability causes his boss to allow him to set up special displays. | Monica loves using her persuasive skills to sell the company's new line of cosmetics. |
| Microbiologist Ann is ecstatic she's identified the viral strain causing a deadly illness. | When Tom wins a very tough court case, he is named junior partner in the firm Biddle & Twiddle. | For perfect work attendance, Herb is presented with an award at the company banquet. | Since Cathy has mastered the art of mixing fertilizers, she is asked to mix all the nursery chemicals. | Nurse Nora thrives on the challenge of working in a big city hospital's emergency room. |
| Chuck takes pleasure in having operated his forklift for three years without an accident. | Larry's willingness to learn from the head chef at Chez's, secures him the job of assistant chef. | For heroic effort in saving a child's life, Fireman George is awarded the "Medal of Valor." | Jan's knack for selecting the right earrings has led to her ordering all earrings at the store. | As a new supervisor in a large print shop, Tom particularly enjoys the role of "coach." |
| George is delighted that he's had no errors in his daily cash drawer reconciliation in over a month. | Judy's adaptability as a substitute postal worker results in a permanent position in a small post office. | Steve is inducted into the company "Hall of Fame" for landing a record number of new accounts. | Joe, a stable hand, displays such an affinity with horses that he is allowed to help groom them. | Ralph finds the wide variety of tasks involved in taking care of Mr. Nabob's estate stimulating. |

# ★ ★ ★ MOTIVATION BINGO ★ ★ ★

| | B | I | N | G | O |
|---|---|---|---|---|---|
| **Achievement** | Now that she has mastered a new filing system, Darlene can proudly find any document in seconds. | Lennie is thrilled that he has reached his sales goal this month. | Zelda is gratified that she can now answer all technical questions about the appliances she sells. | Mike is pleased that he can now present ideas to his firm's top management without appearing nervous. | Martha is elated that she's finished the fine details of the jewelry for the company's spring collection. |
| **Advancement** | Professor Smith at Hardwork University, after writing a best-seller, advances to associate professor. | Keeping her cookie line producing at maximum output, gets Maggie promoted to manager. | Landing the largest new customer in five years gets Walter named account executive. | Darin's quality customer service at the bank has led to his advancement to head teller. | Liz's willingness to handle difficult cases results in her being appointed supervisor of child welfare. |
| **Recognition** | For 10 years of service, Jane gets a brass plaque. | For outstanding sales, Al is congratulated in the company newsletter. | For completing the training course with high marks, Marilyn receives a framed diploma. | As employee of the month, Cecil's picture is in the city newspaper. | For her superior classroom skills, Millie is named "Teacher of the Year." |
| **Responsibility** | Because she has demonstrated patience, Margie now handles complaints in key accounts. | With her upgraded keyboard skills, Barbara is allowed to do typing for company executives. | Because Jeff works so responsibly at the fast-food restaurant, he gets to close for the boss on weekends. | Fred manages his bottling division with such good results his supervisor allows him to do all the hiring. | Diane's proficiency in visualizing results causes her boss to assign her complex floral arrangements. |
| **Work Itself** | Matt thinks that spending his days creating toys is a dream job. | Lydia finds creating new computer software an exciting challenge. | Legal assistant Marilyn finds doing research on a case of particular interest to her fulfilling. | Monty gets to create a company training course that he's wanted to do for five years. | Professor Don is elated about teaching a class on his pet interest, primate socialization. |

# ★ ★ ★ MOTIVATION BINGO ★ ★ ★ ★

| | B | I | N | G | O |
|---|---|---|---|---|---|
| **Achievement** | Lennie is thrilled that he has reached his sales goal this month. | Zelda is gratified that she can now answer all technical questions about the appliances she sells. | Mike is pleased that he can now present ideas to his firm's top management without appearing nervous. | Martha is elated that she's finished the fine details of the jewelry for the company's spring collection. | Wilma, the school custodian, is very happy she can finally control the new floor scrubber. |
| **Advancement** | Keeping her cookie line producing at maximum output, gets Maggie promoted to manager. | Landing the largest new customer in five years gets Walter named account executive. | Darin's quality customer service at the bank has led to his advancement to head teller. | Liz's willingness to handle difficult cases results in her being appointed supervisor of child welfare. | Ben's loyalty to his co-workers gained him his new rank of Sergeant at the Highway Patrol. |
| **Recognition** | For outstanding sales, Al is congratulated in the company newsletter. | For completing the training course with high marks, Marilyn receives a framed diploma. | As employee of the month, Cecil's picture is in the city newspaper. | For her superior classroom skills, Millie is named "Teacher of the Year." | John's creative advertising art is displayed in the agency's office lobby. |
| **Responsibility** | With her upgraded keyboard skills, Barbara is allowed to do typing for company executives. | Because Jeff works so responsibly at the fast-food restaurant, he gets to close for the boss on weekends. | Fred manages his bottling division with such good results his supervisor allows him to do all the hiring. | Diane's proficiency in visualizing results causes her boss to assign her complex floral arrangements. | Phyllis' articles on local events affords her a chance to try her hand at national news stories. |
| **Work Itself** | Lydia finds creating new computer software an exciting challenge. | Legal assistant Marilyn finds doing research on a case of particular interest to her fulfilling. | Monty gets to create a company training course that he's wanted to do for five years. | Professor Don is elated about teaching a class on his pet interest, primate socialization. | Phil enjoys making one-of-a-kind items in a custom machine shop. |

31

# ★ ★ ★ MOTIVATION BINGO ★ ★ ★ ★

|  | B | I | N | G | O |
|---|---|---|---|---|---|
| **Achievement** | Zelda is gratified that she can now answer all technical questions about the appliances she sells. | Mike is pleased that he can now present ideas to his firm's top management without appearing nervous. | Martha is elated that she's finished the fine details of the jewelry for the company's spring collection. | Wilma, the school custodian, is very happy she can finally control the new floor scrubber. | Postmaster Ben is proud he can address 90% of his customers at the Heathville post office by name. |
| **Advancement** | Landing the largest new customer in five years gets Walter named account executive. | Darin's quality customer service at the bank has led to his advancement to head teller. | Liz's willingness to handle difficult cases results in her being appointed supervisor of child welfare. | Ben's loyalty to his co-workers gained him his new rank of Sergeant at the Highway Patrol. | Always willing to help new employees learn necessary skills, Betty is elevated to technical trainer. |
| **Recognition** | For completing the training course with high marks, Marilyn receives a framed diploma. | As employee of the month, Cecil's picture is in the city newspaper. | For her superior classroom skills, Millie is named "Teacher of the Year." | John's creative advertising art is displayed in the agency's office lobby. | For her hard work in researching a cure for Alzheimer's, Mary is asked to address Congress. |
| **Responsibility** | Because Jeff works so responsibly at the fast-food restaurant, he gets to close for the boss on weekends. | Fred manages his bottling division with such good results his supervisor allows him to do all the hiring. | Diane's proficiency in visualizing results causes her boss to assign her complex floral arrangements. | Phyllis' articles on local events affords her a chance to try her hand at national news stories. | Brad's grocery shelving ability causes his boss to allow him to set up special displays. |
| **Work Itself** | Legal assistant Marilyn finds doing research on a case of particular interest to her fulfilling. | Monty gets to create a company training course that he's wanted to do for five years. | Professor Don is elated about teaching a class on his pet interest, primate socialization. | Phil enjoys making one-of-a-kind items in a custom machine shop. | Monica loves using her persuasive skills to sell the company's new line of cosmetics. |

# ★ ★ MOTIVATION BINGO ★ ★ ★

|  | B | I | N | G | O |
|---|---|---|---|---|---|
| **Achievement** | Mike is pleased that he can now present ideas to his firm's top management without appearing nervous. | Martha is elated that she's finished the fine details of the jewelry for the company's spring collection. | Wilma, the school custodian, is very happy she can finally control the new floor scrubber. | Postmaster Ben is proud he can address 90% of his customers at the Heathville post office by name. | Microbiologist Ann is ecstatic she's identified the viral strain causing a deadly illness. |
| **Advancement** | Darin's quality customer service at the bank has led to his advancement to head teller. | Liz's willingness to handle difficult cases results in her being appointed supervisor of child welfare. | Ben's loyalty to his co-workers gained him his new rank of Sergeant at the Highway Patrol. | Always willing to help new employees learn necessary skills, Betty is elevated to technical trainer. | When Tom wins a very tough court case, he is named junior partner in the firm Biddle & Twiddle. |
| **Recognition** | As employee of the month, Cecil's picture is in the city newspaper. | For her superior classroom skills, Millie is named "Teacher of the Year." | John's creative advertising art is displayed in the agency's office lobby. | For her hard work in researching a cure for Alzheimer's, Mary is asked to address Congress. | For perfect work attendance, Herb is presented with an award at the company banquet. |
| **Responsibility** | Fred manages his bottling division with such good results his supervisor allows him to do all the hiring. | Diane's proficiency in visualizing results causes her boss to assign her complex floral arrangements. | Phyllis' articles on local events affords her a chance to try her hand at national news stories. | Brad's grocery shelving ability causes his boss to allow him to set up special displays. | Since Cathy has mastered the art of mixing fertilizers, she is asked to mix all the nursery chemicals. |
| **Work Itself** | Monty gets to create a company training course that he's wanted to do for five years. | Professor Don is elated about teaching a class on his pet interest, primate socialization. | Phil enjoys making one-of-a-kind items in a custom machine shop. | Monica loves using her persuasive skills to sell the company's new line of cosmetics. | Nurse Nora thrives on the challenge of working in a big city hospital's emergency room. |

# ★ ★ ★ MOTIVATION BINGO ★ ★ ★

| | B | I | N | G | O |
|---|---|---|---|---|---|
| **Achievement** | Martha is elated that she's finished the fine details of the jewelry for the company's spring collection. | Wilma, the school custodian, is very happy she can finally control the new floor scrubber. | Postmaster Ben is proud he can address 90% of his customers at the Heathville post office by name. | Microbiologist Ann is ecstatic she's identified the viral strain causing a deadly illness. | Chuck takes pleasure in having operated his forklift for three years without an accident. |
| **Advancement** | Liz's willingness to handle difficult cases results in her being appointed supervisor of child welfare. | Ben's loyalty to his co-workers gained him his new rank of Sergeant at the Highway Patrol. | Always willing to help new employees learn necessary skills, Betty is elevated to technical trainer. | When Tom wins a very tough court case, he is named junior partner in the firm Biddle & Twiddle. | Larry's willingness to learn from the head chef at Chez's, secures him the job of assistant chef. |
| **Recognition** | For her superior classroom skills, Millie is named "Teacher of the Year." | John's creative advertising art is displayed in the agency's office lobby. | For her hard work in researching a cure for Alzheimer's, Mary is asked to address Congress. | For perfect work attendance, Herb is presented with an award at the company banquet. | For heroic effort in saving a child's life, Fireman George is awarded the "Medal of Valor." |
| **Responsibility** | Diane's proficiency in visualizing results causes her boss to assign her complex floral arrangements. | Phyllis' articles on local events affords her a chance to try her hand at national news stories. | Brad's grocery shelving ability causes his boss to allow him to set up special displays. | Since Cathy has mastered the art of mixing fertilizers, she is asked to mix all the nursery chemicals. | Jan's knack for selecting the right earrings has led to her ordering all earrings at the store. |
| **Work Itself** | Professor Don is elated about teaching a class on his pet interest, primate socialization. | Phil enjoys making one-of-a-kind items in a custom machine shop. | Monica loves using her persuasive skills to sell the company's new line of cosmetics. | Nurse Nora thrives on the challenge of working in a big city hospital's emergency room. | As a new supervisor in a large print shop, Tom particularly enjoys the role of "coach." |

# ★ ★ ★ MOTIVATION BINGO ★ ★ ★

| | B | I | N | G | O |
|---|---|---|---|---|---|
| **Achievement** | Wilma, the school custodian, is very happy she can finally control the new floor scrubber. | Postmaster Ben is proud he can address 90% of his customers at the Heathville post office by name. | Microbiologist Ann is ecstatic she's identified the viral strain causing a deadly illness. | Chuck takes pleasure in having operated his forklift for three years without an accident. | George is delighted that he's had no errors in his daily cash drawer reconciliation in over a month. |
| **Advancement** | Ben's loyalty to his co-workers gained him his new rank of Sergeant at the Highway Patrol. | Always willing to help new employees learn necessary skills, Betty is elevated to technical trainer. | When Tom wins a very tough court case, he is named junior partner in the firm Biddle & Twiddle. | Larry's willingness to learn from the head chef at Chez's, secures him the job of assistant chef. | Judy's adaptability as a substitute postal worker results in a permanent position in a small post office. |
| **Recognition** | John's creative advertising art is displayed in the agency's office lobby. | For her hard work in researching a cure for Alzheimer's, Mary is asked to address Congress. | For perfect work attendance, Herb is presented with an award at the company banquet. | For heroic effort in saving a child's life, Fireman George is awarded the "Medal of Valor." | Steve is inducted into the company "Hall of Fame" for landing a record number of new accounts. |
| **Responsibility** | Phyllis' articles on local events affords her a chance to try her hand at national news stories. | Brad's grocery shelving ability causes his boss to allow him to set up special displays. | Since Cathy has mastered the art of mixing fertilizers, she is asked to mix all the nursery chemicals. | Jan's knack for selecting the right earrings has led to her ordering all earrings at the store. | Joe, a stable hand, displays such an affinity with horses that he is allowed to help groom them. |
| **Work Itself** | Phil enjoys making one-of-a-kind items in a custom machine shop. | Monica loves using her persuasive skills to sell the company's new line of cosmetics. | Nurse Nora thrives on the challenge of working in a big city hospital's emergency room. | As a new supervisor in a large print shop, Tom particularly enjoys the role of "coach." | Ralph finds the wide variety of tasks involved in taking care of Mr. Nabob's estate stimulating. |

# ★ ★ ★ MOTIVATION BINGO ★ ★ ★

|  | B | I | N | G | O |
|---|---|---|---|---|---|
| **Achievement** | Postmaster Ben is proud he can address 90% of his customers at the Heathville post office by name. | Microbiologist Ann is ecstatic she's identified the viral strain causing a deadly illness. | Chuck takes pleasure in having operated his forklift for three years without an accident. | George is delighted that he's had no errors in his daily cash drawer reconciliation in over a month. | Now that she has mastered a new filing system, Darlene can proudly find any document in seconds. |
| **Advancement** | Always willing to help new employees learn necessary skills, Betty is elevated to technical trainer. | When Tom wins a very tough court case, he is named junior partner in the firm Biddle & Twiddle. | Larry's willingness to learn from the head chef at Chez's, secures him the job of assistant chef. | Judy's adaptability as a substitute postal worker results in a permanent position in a small post office. | Professor Smith at Hardwork University, after writing a best-seller, advances to associate professor. |
| **Recognition** | For her hard work in researching a cure for Alzheimer's, Mary is asked to address Congress. | For perfect work attendance, Herb is presented with an award at the company banquet. | For heroic effort in saving a child's life, Fireman George is awarded the "Medal of Valor." | Steve is inducted into the company "Hall of Fame" for landing a record number of new accounts. | For 10 years of service, Jane gets a brass plaque. |
| **Responsibility** | Brad's grocery shelving ability causes his boss to allow him to set up special displays. | Since Cathy has mastered the art of mixing fertilizers, she is asked to mix all the nursery chemicals. | Jan's knack for selecting the right earrings has led to her ordering all earrings at the store. | Joe, a stable hand, displays such an affinity with horses that he is allowed to help groom them. | Because she has demonstrated patience, Margie now handles complaints in key accounts. |
| **Work Itself** | Monica loves using her persuasive skills to sell the company's new line of cosmetics. | Nurse Nora thrives on the challenge of working in a big city hospital's emergency room. | As a new supervisor in a large print shop, Tom particularly enjoys the role of "coach." | Ralph finds the wide variety of tasks involved in taking care of Mr. Nabob's estate stimulating. | Matt thinks that spending his days creating toys is a dream job. |

# ★ ★ ★ MOTIVATION BINGO ★ ★ ★

| | B | I | N | G | O |
|---|---|---|---|---|---|
| **Achievement** | Microbiologist Ann is ecstatic she's identified the viral strain causing a deadly illness. | Chuck takes pleasure in having operated his forklift for three years without an accident. | George is delighted that he's had no errors in his daily cash drawer reconciliation in over a month. | Now that she has mastered a new filing system, Darlene can proudly find any document in seconds. | Lennie is thrilled that he has reached his sales goal this month. |
| **Advancement** | When Tom wins a very tough court case, he is named junior partner in the firm Biddle & Twiddle. | Larry's willingness to learn from the head chef at Chez's, secures him the job of assistant chef. | Judy's adaptability as a substitute postal worker results in a permanent position in a small post office. | Professor Smith at Hardwork University, after writing a best-seller, advances to associate professor. | Keeping her cookie line producing at maximum output, gets Maggie promoted to manager. |
| **Recognition** | For perfect work attendance, Herb is presented with an award at the company banquet. | For heroic effort in saving a child's life, Fireman George is awarded the "Medal of Valor." | Steve is inducted into the company "Hall of Fame" for landing a record number of new accounts. | For 10 years of service, Jane gets a brass plaque. | For outstanding sales, Al is congratulated in the company newsletter. |
| **Responsibility** | Since Cathy has mastered the art of mixing fertilizers, she is asked to mix all the nursery chemicals. | Jan's knack for selecting the right earrings has led to her ordering all earrings at the store. | Joe, a stable hand, displays such an affinity with horses that he is allowed to help groom them. | Because she has demonstrated patience, Margie now handles complaints in key accounts. | With her upgraded keyboard skills, Barbara is allowed to do typing for company executives. |
| **Work Itself** | Nurse Nora thrives on the challenge of working in a big city hospital's emergency room. | As a new supervisor in a large print shop, Tom particularly enjoys the role of "coach." | Ralph finds the wide variety of tasks involved in taking care of Mr. Nabob's estate stimulating. | Matt thinks that spending his days creating toys is a dream job. | Lydia finds creating new computer software an exciting challenge. |

# ★ ★ ★ MOTIVATION BINGO ★ ★ ★

|  | B | I | N | G | O |
|---|---|---|---|---|---|
| **Achievement** | Chuck takes pleasure in having operated his forklift for three years without an accident. | George is delighted that he's had no errors in his daily cash drawer reconciliation in over a month. | Now that she has mastered a new filing system, Darlene can proudly find any document in seconds. | Lennie is thrilled that he has reached his sales goal this month. | Zelda is gratified that she can now answer all technical questions about the appliances she sells. |
| **Advancement** | Larry's willingness to learn from the head chef at Chez's, secures him the job of assistant chef. | Judy's adaptability as a substitute postal worker results in a permanent position in a small post office. | Professor Smith at Hardwork University, after writing a best-seller, advances to associate professor. | Keeping her cookie line producing at maximum output, gets Maggie promoted to manager. | Landing the largest new customer in five years gets Walter named account executive. |
| **Recognition** | For heroic effort in saving a child's life, Fireman George is awarded the "Medal of Valor." | Steve is inducted into the company "Hall of Fame" for landing a record number of new accounts. | For 10 years of service, Jane gets a brass plaque. | For outstanding sales, Al is congratulated in the company newsletter. | For completing the training course with high marks, Marilyn receives a framed diploma. |
| **Responsibility** | Jan's knack for selecting the right earrings has led to her ordering all earrings at the store. | Joe, a stable hand, displays such an affinity with horses that he is allowed to help groom them. | Because she has demonstrated patience, Margie now handles complaints in key accounts. | With her upgraded keyboard skills, Barbara is allowed to do typing for company executives. | Because Jeff works so responsibly at the fast-food restaurant, he gets to close for the boss on weekends. |
| **Work Itself** | As a new supervisor in a large print shop, Tom particularly enjoys the role of "coach." | Ralph finds the wide variety of tasks involved in taking care of Mr. Nabob's estate stimulating. | Matt thinks that spending his days creating toys is a dream job. | Lydia finds creating new computer software an exciting challenge. | Legal assistant Marilyn finds doing research on a case of particular interest to her fulfilling. |

# ★★★ MOTIVATION BINGO ★★★

| | B | I | N | G | O |
|---|---|---|---|---|---|
| **Achievement** | George is delighted that he's had no errors in his daily cash drawer reconciliation in over a month. | Now that she has mastered a new filing system, Darlene can proudly find any document in seconds. | Lennie is thrilled that he has reached his sales goal this month. | Zelda is gratified that she can now answer all technical questions about the appliances she sells. | Mike is pleased that he can now present ideas to his firm's top management without appearing nervous. |
| **Advancement** | Judy's adaptability as a substitute postal worker results in a permanent position in a small post office. | Professor Smith at Hardwork University, after writing a best-seller, advances to associate professor. | Keeping her cookie line producing at maximum output, gets Maggie promoted to manager. | Landing the largest new customer in five years gets Walter named account executive. | Darin's quality customer service at the bank has led to his advancement to head teller. |
| **Recognition** | Steve is inducted into the company "Hall of Fame" for landing a record number of new accounts. | For 10 years of service, Jane gets a brass plaque. | For outstanding sales, Al is congratulated in the company newsletter. | For completing the training course with high marks, Marilyn receives a framed diploma. | As employee of the month, Cecil's picture is in the city newspaper. |
| **Responsibility** | Joe, a stable hand, displays such an affinity with horses that he is allowed to help groom them. | Because she has demonstrated patience, Margie now handles complaints in key accounts. | With her upgraded keyboard skills, Barbara is allowed to do typing for company executives. | Because Jeff works so responsibly at the fast-food restaurant, he gets to close for the boss on weekends. | Fred manages his bottling division with such good results his supervisor allows him to do all the hiring. |
| **Work Itself** | Ralph finds the wide variety of tasks involved in taking care of Mr. Nabob's estate stimulating. | Matt thinks that spending his days creating toys is a dream job. | Lydia finds creating new computer software an exciting challenge. | Legal assistant Marilyn finds doing research on a case of particular interest to her fulfilling. | Monty gets to create a company training course that he's wanted to do for five years. |

# ★ ★ ★ MOTIVATION BINGO ★ ★ ★

| | B | I | N | G | O |
|---|---|---|---|---|---|
| **Achievement** | Now that she has mastered a new filing system, Darlene can proudly find any document in seconds. | Lennie is thrilled that he has reached his sales goal this month. | Microbiologist Ann is ecstatic she's identified the viral strain causing a deadly illness. | Chuck takes pleasure in having operated his forklift for three years without an accident. | George is delighted that he's had no errors in his daily cash drawer reconciliation in over a month. |
| **Advancement** | Professor Smith at Hardwork University, after writing a best-seller, advances to associate professor. | Keeping her cookie line producing at maximum output, gets Maggie promoted to manager. | When Tom wins a very tough court case, he is named junior partner in the firm Biddle & Twiddle. | Larry's willingness to learn from the head chef at Chez's, secures him the job of assistant chef. | Judy's adaptability as a substitute postal worker results in a permanent position in a small post office. |
| **Recognition** | For 10 years of service, Jane gets a brass plaque. | For outstanding sales, Al is congratulated in the company newsletter. | For perfect work attendance, Herb is presented with an award at the company banquet. | For heroic effort in saving a child's life, Fireman George is awarded the "Medal of Valor." | Steve is inducted into the company "Hall of Fame" for landing a record number of new accounts. |
| **Responsibility** | Because she has demonstrated patience, Margie now handles complaints in key accounts. | With her upgraded keyboard skills, Barbara is allowed to do typing for company executives. | Since Cathy has mastered the art of mixing fertilizers, she is asked to mix all the nursery chemicals. | Jan's knack for selecting the right earrings has led to her ordering all earrings at the store. | Joe, a stable hand, displays such an affinity with horses that he is allowed to help groom them. |
| **Work Itself** | Matt thinks that spending his days creating toys is a dream job. | Lydia finds creating new computer software an exciting challenge. | Nurse Nora thrives on the challenge of working in a big city hospital's emergency room. | As a new supervisor in a large print shop, Tom particularly enjoys the role of "coach." | Ralph finds the wide variety of tasks involved in taking care of Mr. Nabob's estate stimulating. |

# ★★ MOTIVATION BINGO ★★★★

|  | B | I | N | G | O |
|---|---|---|---|---|---|
| **Achievement** | Zelda is gratified that she can now answer all technical questions about the appliances she sells. | Mike is pleased that he can now present ideas to his firm's top management without appearing nervous. | Martha is elated that she's finished the fine details of the jewelry for the company's spring collection. | Postmaster Ben is proud he can address 90% of his customers at the Heathville post office by name. | Microbiologist Ann is ecstatic she's identified the viral strain causing a deadly illness. |
| **Advancement** | Landing the largest new customer in five years gets Walter named account executive. | Darin's quality customer service at the bank has led to his advancement to head teller. | Liz's willingness to handle difficult cases results in her being appointed supervisor of child welfare. | Always willing to help new employees learn necessary skills, Betty is elevated to technical trainer. | When Tom wins a very tough court case, he is named junior partner in the firm Biddle & Twiddle. |
| **Recognition** | For completing the training course with high marks, Marilyn receives a framed diploma. | As employee of the month, Cecil's picture is in the city newspaper. | For her superior classroom skills, Millie is named "Teacher of the Year." | For her hard work in researching a cure for Alzheimer's, Mary is asked to address Congress. | For perfect work attendance, Herb is presented with an award at the company banquet. |
| **Responsibility** | Because Jeff works so responsibly at the fast-food restaurant, he gets to close for the boss on weekends. | Fred manages his bottling division with such good results his supervisor allows him to do all the hiring. | Diane's proficiency in visualizing results causes her boss to assign her complex floral arrangements. | Brad's grocery shelving ability causes his boss to allow him to set up special displays. | Since Cathy has mastered the art of mixing fertilizers, she is asked to mix all the nursery chemicals. |
| **Work Itself** | Legal assistant Marilyn finds doing research on a case of particular interest to her fulfilling. | Monty gets to create a company training course that he's wanted to do for five years. | Professor Don is elated about teaching a class on his pet interest, primate socialization. | Monica loves using her persuasive skills to sell the company's new line of cosmetics. | Nurse Nora thrives on the challenge of working in a big city hospital's emergency room. |

41

# ★ ★ ★ MOTIVATION BINGO ★ ★ ★

| | B | I | N | G | O |
|---|---|---|---|---|---|
| **Achievement** | Now that she has mastered a new filing system, Darlene can proudly find any document in seconds. | Zelda is gratified that she can now answer all technical questions about the appliances she sells. | Martha is elated that she's finished the fine details of the jewelry for the company's spring collection. | Postmaster Ben is proud he can address 90% of his customers at the Heathville post office by name. | Chuck takes pleasure in having operated his forklift for three years without an accident. |
| **Advancement** | Professor Smith at Hardwork University, after writing a best-seller, advances to associate professor. | Landing the largest new customer in five years gets Walter named account executive. | Liz's willingness to handle difficult cases results in her being appointed supervisor of child welfare. | Always willing to help new employees learn necessary skills, Betty is elevated to technical trainer. | Larry's willingness to learn from the head chef at Chez's, secures him the job of assistant chef. |
| **Recognition** | For 10 years of service, Jane gets a brass plaque. | For completing the training course with high marks, Marilyn receives a framed diploma. | For her superior classroom skills, Millie is named "Teacher of the Year." | For her hard work in researching a cure for Alzheimer's, Mary is asked to address Congress. | For heroic effort in saving a child's life, Fireman George is awarded the "Medal of Valor." |
| **Responsibility** | Because she has demonstrated patience, Margie now handles complaints in key accounts. | Because Jeff works so responsibly at the fast-food restaurant, he gets to close for the boss on weekends. | Diane's proficiency in visualizing results causes her boss to assign her complex floral arrangements. | Brad's grocery shelving ability causes his boss to allow him to set up special displays. | Jan's knack for selecting the right earrings has led to her ordering all earrings at the store. |
| **Work Itself** | Matt thinks that spending his days creating toys is a dream job. | Legal assistant Marilyn finds doing research on a case of particular interest to her fulfilling. | Professor Don is elated about teaching a class on his pet interest, primate socialization. | Monica loves using her persuasive skills to sell the company's new line of cosmetics. | As a new supervisor in a large print shop, Tom particularly enjoys the role of "coach." |

# ★ ★ ★ MOTIVATION BINGO ★ ★ ★

| | B | I | N | G | O |
|---|---|---|---|---|---|
| **Achievement** | Lennie is thrilled that he has reached his sales goal this month. | Mike is pleased that he can now present ideas to his firm's top management without appearing nervous. | Wilma, the school custodian, is very happy she can finally control the new floor scrubber. | Microbiologist Ann is ecstatic she's identified the viral strain causing a deadly illness. | George is delighted that he's had no errors in his daily cash drawer reconciliation in over a month. |
| **Advancement** | Keeping her cookie line producing at maximum output, gets Maggie promoted to manager. | Darin's quality customer service at the bank has led to his advancement to head teller. | Ben's loyalty to his co-workers gained him his new rank of Sergeant at the Highway Patrol. | When Tom wins a very tough court case, he is named junior partner in the firm Biddle & Twiddle. | Judy's adaptability as a substitute postal worker results in a permanent position in a small post office. |
| **Recognition** | For outstanding sales, Al is congratulated in the company newsletter. | As employee of the month, Cecil's picture is in the city newspaper. | John's creative advertising art is displayed in the agency's office lobby. | For perfect work attendance, Herb is presented with an award at the company banquet. | Steve is inducted into the company "Hall of Fame," for landing a record number of new accounts. |
| **Responsibility** | With her upgraded keyboard skills, Barbara is allowed to do typing for company executives. | Fred manages his bottling division with such good results his supervisor allows him to do all the hiring. | Phyllis' articles on local events affords her a chance to try her hand at national news stories. | Since Cathy has mastered the art of mixing fertilizers, she is asked to mix all the nursery chemicals. | Joe, a stable hand, displays such an affinity with horses that he is allowed to help groom them. |
| **Work Itself** | Lydia finds creating new computer software an exciting challenge. | Monty gets to create a company training course that he's wanted to do for five years. | Phil enjoys making one-of-a-kind items in a custom machine shop. | Nurse Nora thrives on the challenge of working in a big city hospital's emergency room. | Ralph finds the wide variety of tasks involved in taking care of Mr. Nabob's estate stimulating. |

# ★ ★ ★ MOTIVATION BINGO ★ ★ ★

|  | B | I | N | G | O |
|---|---|---|---|---|---|
| **Achievement** | Lennie is thrilled that he has reached his sales goal this month. | Martha is elated that she's finished the fine details of the jewelry for the company's spring collection. | Postmaster Ben is proud he can address 90% of his customers at the Heathville post office by name. | Microbiologist Ann is ecstatic she's identified the viral strain causing a deadly illness. | Chuck takes pleasure in having operated his forklift for three years without an accident. |
| **Advancement** | Keeping her cookie line producing at maximum output, Maggie promoted to manager. | Liz's willingness to handle difficult cases results in her being appointed supervisor of child welfare. | Always willing to help new employees learn necessary skills, Betty is elevated to technical trainer. | When Tom wins a very tough court case, he is named junior partner in the firm Biddle & Twiddle. | Larry's willingness to learn from the head chef at Chez's, secures him the job of assistant chef. |
| **Recognition** | For outstanding sales, Al is congratulated in the company newsletter. | For her superior classroom skills, Millie is named "Teacher of the Year." | For her hard work in researching a cure for Alzheimer's, Mary is asked to address Congress. | For perfect work attendance, Herb is presented with an award at the company banquet. | For heroic effort in saving a child's life, Fireman George is awarded the "Medal of Valor." |
| **Responsibility** | With her upgraded keyboard skills, Barbara is allowed to do typing for company executives. | Diane's proficiency in visualizing results causes her boss to assign her complex floral arrangements. | Brad's grocery shelving ability causes his boss to allow him to set up special displays. | Since Cathy has mastered the art of mixing fertilizers, she is asked to mix all the nursery chemicals. | Jan's knack for selecting the right earrings has led to her ordering all earrings at the store. |
| **Work Itself** | Lydia finds creating new computer software an exciting challenge. | Professor Dan is elated about teaching a class on his pet interest, primate socialization. | Monica loves using her persuasive skills to sell the company's new line of cosmetics. | Nurse Nora thrives on the challenge of working in a big city hospital's emergency room. | As a new supervisor in a large print shop, Tom particularly enjoys the role of "coach." |

# ★ ★ ★ MOTIVATION BINGO ★ ★ ★

|  | B | I | N | G | O |
|---|---|---|---|---|---|
| **Achievement** | Free Space | | | | Free Space |
| **Advancement** | | Free Space | | Free Space | |
| **Recognition** | Free Space | Free Space | Free Space | | |
| **Responsibility** | | | | Free Space | |
| **Work Itself** | Free Space | | | | Free Space |

# PLEASE PASS THE RISKETTS

| | |
|---|---|
| **TOPIC** | Acceptable and unacceptable risks |

Most companies limit the risks employees are allowed to take. Companies that allow workers to take unbridled risks can reap a harvest of employee accidents, lawsuits, and financial ruin. On the other hand, organizations that permit employees to go forward only with a "sure thing" can lose out to competitors when it comes to bringing new products and services to market. Eventually, the company may lose market share and go out of business due to obsolete products and practices. The learning organization encourages employees to engage in appropriate risk taking. Workers are made aware of what are considered "appropriate" and "inappropriate" risks. Because risk taking is viewed as essential to keeping the company on the cutting edge and employees in a continuous personal mastery mode, it is rewarded even when results do not turn out as hoped.

To assess the types of risks an organization considers appropriate, it is often helpful to look at three types of risks. First there are the "unacceptable risks." They are not to be taken under any circumstances. Second, there are the "acceptable if risks." These risks are only OK to take when good results ensue. Finally, there are the "acceptable risks." These risks are almost always acceptable regardless of the outcome.

| | |
|---|---|
| **LEARNING OBJECTIVE** | Participants will be able to engage in appropriate risk taking. |
| **NUMBER OF PARTICIPANTS** | Any number divided into groups of 9, 12, or 15 players |
| **PLAYING TIME** | 20-25 minutes depending upon the number of players |
| **REQUIRED MATERIALS** | A set of the Risk Cards for every three players, flip chart, and markers |
| **TO PLAY** | 1. Introduce players to the concept of three kinds of workplace risks (i.e., unacceptable under any circumstances, acceptable only when good results |

ensue, and almost always acceptable regardless of the outcome).

2. Go over the learning objective for the game.

3. Tell players that they are about to engage in a game which requires them to distinguish between three kinds of risks. At various times during the game they will be handed Risk Cards and asked to select from the cards a risk which is unacceptable under any circumstances, a risk which is acceptable only when good results ensue, or a risk which is almost always acceptable regardless of the outcome.

4. Explain that they will earn points only when their selection of a risk is in agreement with other members of their team.

5. Divide the larger group into two or three subgroups. If there are only nine players, have them form three parallel rows of three players each facing the front of the room with approximately two feet of space between the rows. If there are 12 players, form three rows of four participants each. If there are 15 players, form three rows of five persons each.

6. Inform players that each row constitutes a team.

7. Advise players that you are about to hand each player in the first row a set of five Risk Cards. Members of the first row (i.e., team one) will carefully read each of the cards and pull out a risk which is "unacceptable under any circumstances" at their place of work. When the facilitator calls "Please pass the risketts," row one will then pass the remaining four Risk Cards back to row two. Row two will read over the remaining four Risk Cards very carefully and pull out a card with a risk which is "acceptable only when good results ensue." Again when the facilitator calls out "Please pass the risketts," row two will pass the remaining three cards back to row three. Members of row three will read the remaining three cards, pull out a risk which is "almost always acceptable regardless of the outcome," and discard the remaining two cards by handing them to the facilitator.

8. Give a set of Risk Cards for round one to the first person in each row.

9. Ask them to pull out a card with a risk which would be "unacceptable under any circumstances."

10. Call out "Please pass the risketts." Direct members of row two to pull out a card with a risk which is "acceptable only when good results ensue."

11. Call out "Please pass the risketts." Ask members in row three to pull out a risk which is "almost always acceptable regardless of the outcome."
12. Collect the discards from row three.
13. Have members of row one read the risks on their cards. Depending upon the number of players on each team (i.e., three, four, or five), award team one a point if two out of three, three out of four, or four out of five selected the same risk.
14. Repeat step 13 for rows two and three.
15. For the second round of play have the teams rotate positions. Have row three move up to row one's position, row one move back to row two's position, and row two move to row three's position.
16. Proceed with round two by recycling through steps 8 to 15. Only this time use the set of Risk Cards designated for round two.
17. Using the set of Risk Cards for round three, repeat steps 8 to 15.
18. Add up the total number of points earned by each team. Declare the team(s) with the most points the winner(s).
19. Debrief players. Have employees gauge their ability to differentiate between what their employer considers "appropriate" and "inappropriate" risk taking. On a flip chart, list forces within an organization that can encourage and discourage risk taking. Ask participants to recall an important lesson they learned when taking a major risk. Have them discuss how the freedom or the lack of freedom to take risks has impacted on individual learning in their company. Request that they share ideas on how appropriate risk taking should be rewarded.

**VARIATION**

Play the game according to the above instructions using your own risk-taking cards. You may also play a simplified version of the game. Prior to playing the simplified version of the game, mark each of the risk cards "unacceptable," "acceptable," or "acceptable if." If possible, base your markings on the opinions of an upper-level manager in the organization for which most of the participants work. Have three teams come forward, one team at a time, and face the audience. One card at a time, read the risk cards for round one to the first team. Ask players to move to their left if they believe a risk is "unacceptable." Have them move to their right if the risk is "acceptable if." Request that they remain in the middle if the risk is "always acceptable." Have those with incorrect answers sit and have those with correct answers move back to, or remain in, the middle position. Continue the process by reading the remaining cards. Compute the first team's score by tallying the number of players who remain standing. Follow the same procedure for teams two and three using round two cards for team two and round three cards for team three. The group having the largest number of standing members becomes the winner. Debrief the players as you did in the original version of this game.

**FOR MORE INFORMATION**

Kline, P. & Saunders, B. (1993). *Ten steps to a learning organization.* Arlington, VA: Great Ocean Publishers, Inc.

# Risk Cards For Round One

To prepare a deck of Risk Cards for round one, photocopy the following items on card-stock paper and cut them out. Use one set of cards for each three players.

| | |
|---|---|
| Give a new customer big credit, trusting that the money will be paid on time. | Purchase a few materials from a cheaper supplier whose products you've never tried. |
| Grossly inflate your accomplishments to get promoted. | Hire a personal friend over applicants better qualified, while keeping your friendship a secret from your supervisor. |

Promise to make quick delivery of products when the materials needed to make them are back-ordered.

## Risk Cards For Round Two

To prepare a deck of Risk Cards for round two, photocopy the following items on card-stock paper and cut them out. Use one set of cards for each three players.

| | |
|---|---|
| Take a potential large-volume customer to dinner at an untried restaurant. | Engage in a romantic relationship with the boss's spouse. |
| Assign a very important task to an outstanding employee even though she or he has never done it before. | Use your own creative graphics for a sales promotion without getting the boss's permission. |

Stop a subordinate from operating equipment when she or he refuses to follow safety rules.

## Risk Cards For Round Three

To prepare a deck of Risk Cards for round three, photocopy the following items on card-stock paper and cut them out. Use one set of cards for each three players.

| | |
|---|---|
| Invite a coworker of the opposite sex to lunch to discuss a business problem. | Leak a story to media about the company's important research breakthrough. |
| Make official public statements about the performance of your company's product which can't be proven. | Tell other customers about the business problems of one of your customers. |

Ship similar products to customers when the exact ones they order are out of stock.

# RISK STYLE DECODER

**TOPIC**

The relationship between the level of risk and the amount of time taken to decide on whether to take the risk

Taking risks is a part of everyday life. Sometimes people voluntarily take a risk (e.g., purchase a state lottery ticket). On other occasions, risks may be forced upon them (e.g., having a dangerous operation that the family doctor claims is needed). Some risks are "low risks" such as in the case of purchasing a lottery ticket. The potential for major harm is low. Other risks may be "high risks" such as in the case of a dangerous operation. The amount of thought individuals give to low and high risks varies according to the level of the risk being considered. Such differences in thought patterns constitute a person's risk-taking style. Personal mastery requires that employees willingly take on significant risks. However, these risks are taken only after careful thought.

**LEARNING OBJECTIVE**

Participants will be able to allot the amount of time given particular risks in proportion to the level of risk being considered.

**NUMBER OF PARTICIPANTS**

Any number

**PLAYING TIME**

12-28 minutes

**REQUIRED MATERIALS**

Pencils, Risk Styles Sheets, a deck of Personal Risk Cards, flip chart, and markers

**TO PLAY**

1. Introduce players to the concept of levels of risk and the amount of thought given to taking risks.
2. Go over the learning objective for the game.
3. Pass out a pencil, Risk Styles Sheet, and deck of Personal Risk Cards to each player.
4. Read aloud the various styles of risk taking listed at the top of the Risk Styles Sheet. Have participants check (√) the type which best describes them.
5. Instruct participants to fold the top portion of their decoder sheet under along the dotted line. Only the

bottom portion of the decoder sheet should be visible.

6. Ask players to record on their Personal Risk Cards the eight most significant risks they have taken during the past 10 years. Each card should contain only one risk.

7. Tell players to stack each of their risk cards in the appropriate square on their Risk Styles Grid.

8. Ask participants to add up the number of risk cards they have placed in each quadrant of the Risk Styles Grid. This number should be recorded to the left or right of each quadrant.

9. Have players compare the risk taking style they said most characterized them at the outset of the game (recorded on folded portion of worksheet) to the quadrant containing the most risk cards. The top right square represents the Jimmy the Greek style, the top left the Evel Knievel style, the bottom right the Mr. Rogers style, and the bottom left the Olive Oyl style.

10. Request that players whose checked (√) risk style is the same as the quadrant in which they placed the most risk cards stand. Declare them winners.

11. Debrief players. Ask players to what degree they believe the risk-taking style they arrived at by placing risk cards on a matrix represents their typical risk-taking style. Have them discuss the kinds of risks which provoked the greatest amount of thought. Request that they compare these risks to risks which involved almost no thought. Ask participants to compare their risk-taking behaviors as individuals at work to their risk-taking behaviors as members of work teams. Do they tend to take higher risks or more risks as team members? Why or why not? Using a flip chart, make a list of Ten Commandments for effective risk taking.

**VARIATION**    Instead of handing players a set of blank Personal Risk Cards, provide them with a preprinted set of cards containing examples of typical workplace risks. Examples might include "You accept a new position that has typically been held by a member of the opposite gender" and "You publicly disagree with your supervisor in the presence of his superiors." Debrief the players as you did in the original version of this game.

**FOR MORE INFORMATION**     Carney, R. (1971) *Risk-taking behavior: Concepts, methods, and applications to smoking and drug abuse.* Springfield, IL: Charles C. Thomas.

## Personal Risk Cards

To prepare a deck of Personal Risk Cards, photocopy the following items on card-stock paper and cut them out.

# Risk Styles Sheets

**Directions**: Check (√) the risk-taking style which best describes your risk-taking behavior.

❑  Jimmy the Greek:   Takes high risks and gives each careful thought.
❑  Evel Knievel:        Takes high risks but does not spend much time thinking about them.
❑  Mr. Rogers:          Takes low risks and carefully thinks about each one.
❑  Olive Oyl:            Takes low risks but spends very little time thinking about them.

---

**Directions**:   Place each of your eight Personal Risk Cards in one of the following squares of the grid.

|  |  |
|---|---|
| **High Risk<br>Given Little<br>Thought** | **High Risk<br>Given Much<br>Thought** |
| **Low Risk<br>Given Little<br>Thought** | **Low Risk<br>Given Much<br>Thought** |

# RUNON REWARDS

**TOPIC**

Rewarding personal mastery

It is generally agreed by most managers that employees will do the things for which they are rewarded. The same holds true for getting employees to engage in personal learning initiatives that challenge their mental abilities. It has therefore become common practice for managers to give employees rewards for engaging in desired behaviors (e.g., salary increases, promotions, and special awards). A major challenge for companies is to come up with reward systems that most effectively reinforce desired behavioral changes. It is not unusual for an organization to discover that some of its rewards encourage behaviors contradictory to those it is trying to promote.

**LEARNING OBJECTIVE**

Participants will be able to identify ways employees can be rewarded for outstanding performance.

**NUMBER OF PARTICIPANTS**

Any number divided into groups of five or six members each

**PLAYING TIME**

10-12 minutes

**REQUIRED MATERIALS**

Pencils, paper, flip chart, and markers

**TO PLAY**

1. Discuss the importance and desirability of rewarding employees for taking on demanding learning initiatives.
2. Go over the learning objective for the game.
3. Explain to participants that they are going to separate into small groups of five or six players and engage in a contest to see which group can come up with the greatest number of rewards.
4. Tell players that there is one "catch" to the game. Except for when the very first reward is written down, all other rewards must begin with the last letter of the previously recorded reward. For example, if one person writes down "money" as the first reward, the next reward on the list must begin with the letter "y." An acceptable answer might be "Yellowstone Park vacation."

5. Divide the larger group into small groups of five or six players.
6. Provide each group with a pencil and a sheet of paper.
7. Explain that the group that properly records the greatest number of rewards will become the winner of the game. Advise players that they have five minutes to compose their list.
8. Give participants five minutes to complete their lists.
9. Determine which group has the most correctly recorded rewards. Declare it the winning group.
10. Debrief players. Make a list of some of the "best rewards" given in the various groups. Place the rewards into three to six categories according to a classification scheme devised by participants. Discuss the types or categories of rewards most suited for reinforcing individual learning initiatives. Debate the proposition that "learning is its own reward."

**VARIATION**

Divide the group into two smaller groups, one on the left side of the room and the other on the right side of the room. Place a flip chart and markers on both sides. When you say "go" have members from the respective sides come forward one at a time to record RunOn rewards on their respective flip charts. Only one person on a team can be out of her or his seat at any given time. A player must first return to her/his seat and be seated before a teammate can come forward to record the next reward. The first team to correctly write ten RunOn rewards is declared the winner. Debrief players as you did in the original version of the game.

**FOR MORE INFORMATION**

Nelson, R. (1994). *1001 ways to reward employees*. New York: Workman Publishing Company, Inc.

# SMART ACTS

| | |
|---|---|
| **TOPIC** | Exemplary learning organizations |
| | Several nationally known companies (e.g., Corning, Kodak, J. P. Morgan, and Motorola) have taken Peter Senge's concepts of a learning organization to heart. They have expended a substantial amount of time and money on mastering the "five disciplines." The open learning cultures they have created might serve as models for other organizations aspiring to become more effective learning organizations. |
| **LEARNING OBJECTIVE** | Participants will be able to cite examples of learning organizations. |
| **NUMBER OF PARTICIPANTS** | Any number divided into two teams |
| **PLAYING TIME** | 15-20 minutes |
| **REQUIRED MATERIALS** | Company Clue Cards, Smart Acts Cards, a pair of socks, flip chart, and markers |

**TO PLAY**

1. Familiarize participants with the concept of the learning organization (see Chapter One). Explain that several nationally known companies have succeeded in becoming learning organizations (do not mention the names of any companies).
2. Go over the learning objective for the game.
3. Explain to players that they are going to divide into two teams and compete in a brief contest. Teams will earn points by correctly identifying companies that are recognized as learning organizations.
4. Divide participants into two competing teams, and ask one contestant from each team to come forward.
5. Advise the two contestants that you will read a card containing several clues. Explain that the team whose representative calls out the correct answer first receives a point; then two new contestants will come forward.
6. If either contestant calls out an incorrect answer, the remaining clues on the card are to be read and the opponent gets a chance at answering.

7. Tell participants that in the event that neither of the contestants answers correctly, they have a second chance to earn a point through a Smart Act Contest. In such cases, the nature of the contest will be read aloud, players will compete, and the winner's team will receive a point.

8. In all, five contestants from each side will come forward to represent their teams. (After one pair of contestants has had an opportunity to compete, they are to take their seats and two new contestants come forward.)

9. Slowly read the first clue card aloud to the contestants.

10. Award a point to the first contestant to give the name of the correct company. If an incorrect answer is given, provide the opponent with an opportunity to answer the question.

11. If neither contestant wins a point, read a Smart Act in which they can compete. Award one point to the winning team.

12. Repeat Steps 9 to 11 for four more pairs of contestants (i.e., one from each team).

13. At the end of five rounds declare the team with the most points the winning team.

14. Debrief players. Ask participants to identify companies in their geographical region or industry that they believe are true learning organizations. List on a flip chart some of the reasons they believe these are learning organizations. Ask players if they think their company is a learning organization. Why or why not?

**VARIATION**

Divide the large group into two competing teams. Read each Smart Clue Card aloud one clue at a time. The first team to correctly identify the learning organization named on the card receives a point. If neither team correctly identifies a company, one contestant from each side comes forward to participate in a Smart Act competition.

**FOR MORE INFORMATION**

Wick, C. W. & Leon, L. S. (1993). *The learning edge: How smart managers and smart companies stay ahead.* New York: McGraw-Hill.

# Company Clue Cards

## KODAK

1. I am a 110+-year-old company based in Rochester, NY.
2. I have developed a center in a restored turn-of-the-century building in Camden, ME, to bring together creative thinkers in electronic imaging.
3. You might say everything about me is based on "vision."
4. Sometimes I roll along or speed by with a flash.
5. You might find my products in a yellow box.
6. I am : 1) Kraft, 2) Eastman Kodak, or 3) Polaroid.

## J. P. MORGAN

1. My customers include corporations worldwide.
2. My success is due to my culture which includes a 3-month training program for all new employees, giving them a sense of investment in me.
3. I am an elite international company based on Wall Street in New York.
4. Rich people come to me, but not for a Visa Card or a car loan.
5. I don't sing for my money like the lady with the same name as mine.
6. I am: 1) J. P. Morgan, Inc. 2) Price Waterhouse, or 3) Chase.

## BOEING

1. I am a Seattle-based company who is the state's as well as the industry's largest employer.
2. My loyal employees are proud of what they do and many celebrate 25 to 45+ years with me.
3. I am the United State's second largest exporter, and you will find my products all over the world.
4. I accidentally made the front page more often than most companies in the '80s, the worst coming in 1985.
5. You might say my products are "high fliers," and I hope they remain there.
6. I am: 1) American Airlines, 2) Boeing, or 3) McDonnell Douglas

---

### CORNING

1. I am a company based in the state of New York with 100+ other sites all over the world.
2. I believe that a competitive edge is attained more by a company's culture than its technology.
3. My chairman's 1983 "10-year vision" has been very successful.
4. My innovative diversity and family-friendly efforts have helped more minorities and women break through the glass ceiling.
5. You might find my break-resistant products atop a power pole or on your dinner table.
6. I am 1) 3M, 2) Tupperware, or 3) Corning.

---

### MOTOROLA

1. I am a 60+-year-old company that makes high-tech electronics.
2. All of my major groups and sectors have benchmarking systems to compare my products with those of competitors.
3. I have a highly successful executive development program.
4. I made the first car radio in 1930, the first two-way mobile radio in 1940, and got the Malcolm Baldridge Award in 1988.
5. I now specialize in products such as microprocessors and brake systems.
6. I am: 1) Motorola, 2) IBM, or 3) GTE.

# Smart Acts

Bumble Bee Buzz-Off

Contestants make a bee-like buzzing sound with their mouths. The one who buzzes the longest without taking a breath becomes the winner.

Grasshopper Hop Along

Contests hop across the room like grasshoppers. The one who touches the opposite wall first is the winner.

Ho, Ho Holler

The first contestant says, "Ho." The second contestant responds with "Ho, ho." The first contestant says "Ho, ho, ho." Play continues with each contestant adding another "Ho." The first person to smile or laugh loses.

One Legged Stand-Up

Without touching anything else in the room, contestants stand only on their left legs. The individual who stands the longest becomes the winner.

Sock It to Me Stand Off

Each contestant puts a pair of socks on her or his hands. When the facilitator says "Go," both people remove the socks and attempt to hit the other in the head with one of the socks by throwing them at the other person. The first player to do so becomes the winner.

Super Spin Around

Contestants spin themselves three turns in a clockwise direction, three turns in a counterclockwise direction, and again three complete turns in a clockwise direction. The first to finish is the winner.

# Chapter Three

# Meta Learning Games

# ACTION FIGURES

| | |
|---|---|
| **TOPIC** | Experiential learning |

According to learning theorist David Kolb, individuals learn and solve problems through a cyclical learning process consisting of four stages. The process begins with a concrete experience (e.g., When Jane restarts her computer after a power outage, she finds a large part of the quarterly report she was writing is missing). The concrete experience is followed by observation and time reflection (e.g., On closer inspection, Jane sees that all of the sections written last are gone; she recalls that the material had not been saved in over an hour). The reflections in turn lead to the formation of generalizations (e.g. Jane thinks that to avoid doing a lot of work on the computer after unexpected power outages, it would be better to save work more often). The learner then tests the generalization and forms a new hypothesis (e.g., Jane saves work after every page written; the next time there is a power outage, a lot less work is lost. Consequently, she saves all future computer work much more frequently).

**LEARNING**

Participants will be able to apply the experiential learning model in a new learning situation.

**NUMBER OF PARTICIPANTS**

Any number divided into groups of five or six players each (all groups must have the same number of players)

**PLAYING TIME**

15-20 minutes

**REQUIRED MATERIALS**

Hula hoops, name cards, straight pins, a watch with a secondhand, paper, and pencils

**TO PLAY**

1. Explain Kolb's Experiential Learning Model to participants.
2. Go over the learning objective for the game.
3. Inform participants that they will be divided into groups and be asked to solve a problem using Kolb's Experiential Learning Model. The goal is to be the group that best solves the problem. In this case it will be the group which is able to complete an assigned task in the shortest period of time.

4. Advise players that when they get into their small groups they will be given a name card to pin on. This is the character they are to play in the game.

5. Inform players that each group will also be given one hula hoop. For the purpose of the game, the hula hoop is to be referred to as the "energizer ring."

6. Divide players into teams of five or six members each. Have teams position themselves around the room at least six to eight feet apart.

7. Supply each group with a set of name cards, straight pins, and one hula hoop.

8. Direct players to pin on their name cards and to form a small circle.

9. Explain to players that they are action figures who are called upon to do good in the world. However, they must first be energized each morning before they go out to fight evil. The only way they can become energized is to pass their entire body through the center of the energizer ring.

10. Advise players that the group which takes the least amount of time being energized is also the group which has the most time left over during any given day to do good. Therefore, the goal of the game is to learn how to become energized in the shortest period of time.

11. Have each team designate one of its members (a person wearing a watch with a secondhand) as its official timekeeper.

12 Provide timekeepers with paper and pencil to record their times.

13 Direct each team to energize themselves. Afterwards direct timekeepers to record their group's times. Have the timekeepers write "trial one" on a piece of paper with how many seconds it took their team to energize itself. In order for groups to compare energizing times, ask timekeepers to read their times aloud.

14. Ask the teams to take one minute to reflect on their energizing experiences. Have them share their individual observations of what happened.

15. Tell teams to take one minute to form generalizations (new concepts) about the energizing process.

16. Give teams 20 seconds to select a generalization about the energizing process that they would like to test.

17. Repeat steps 13 to 16 two or three more times. However, as teams attempt to energize themselves,

have them test hypotheses generated from earlier trials.

18. At the end of the last timing, declare the group(s) with the shortest energizing time(s) the winner(s).

19. Debrief players. Have groups compare the energizing time of their last trial to that of their first. Have them account for the tremendous improvement in time. Have participants share instances in which they have used a learning process similar to that of Kolb's to solve a problem. Ask players to give their opinions as to whether they believe the experiential learning model works equally as well on an individual basis as it does in groups. Discuss whether employees in most organizations possess the skills needed (i.e., reflecting, generalizing, hypothesizing, hypothesis testing) to effectively engage in experiential learning.

**VARIATION**     Have players come up with problems or initiatives to solve. Play the game according to the above directions.

**FOR MORE**
**INFORMATION**     Kolb, D. A., Rubin, I. M., & McIntyre, J. M. (1974). *Organizational psychology: An experiential approach* (2nd ed.). Englewood Cliffs, NJ: Prentice-Hall, Inc.

## Name Cards

To make one set of Action Figure Name Cards, photocopy the following items on card-stock paper and cut them out.

| | |
|---|---|
| **Bad News Badger** | **Disco Dolphin** |
| **Fearless Feline** | **Kung Fu Chicken** |
| **Muscle Mouse** | **Torpedo Turtle** |

# DO IT MYSELF

**TOPIC**

Self-directed learning

Self-directed learning is any systematic learning arrangement in which the learner, not an instructor, assumes full responsibility for the learning. It is the learner who decides what will be learned, the pace at which the learning will proceed, and the means by which the learning will be accomplished (i.e., the learning strategies to be employed). The learner may call upon instructors, tutors, mentors, resource people, supervisors, coworkers, and peers for assistance. Self-directed learning is strongly advocated by many adult educators.

**LEARNING OBJECTIVE**

Participants will be able to assess how self-directing they would prefer their employee training and education to be.

**NUMBER OF PARTICIPANTS**

Any number divided into pairs (preferably players who know one another)

**PLAYING TIME**

10-15 minutes

**REQUIRED MATERIALS**

A set of Learning Choice Cards, pencils, flip chart, and markers

**TO PLAY**

1. Explain to participants the concept of self-directed learning.
2. Go over the learning objective of the game.
3. Inform participants that they are about to play a game in which they will be asked to predict the preferred learning mode of another player.
4. Have participants pair up with someone they know or someone who is in the same line of work.
5. Provide each pair a set of materials (i.e., a pencil and set of Learning Choice Cards).
6. Request that one of the partners deal five cards each to her or his partner and herself or himself.
7. Explain that participants are to carefully read the cards they have been dealt. Afterwards they are to place an "x" in either the DIM box (i.e., self-directed learning box) or the FT box (i.e., formal training

box) based on what they believe to be their partner's preferred learning mode. If players believe their partner would prefer to achieve the stated learning on their own through self-directed learning strategies, they should check the DIM box. If players believe their partner would prefer to accomplish the stated learning by attending formal training classes, they should check the FT box.

8. Advise players that play begins with one person reading her or his cards to her or his partner. Whenever a card is read containing a type of learning the partner would prefer to do in a self-directed mode, she or he is to shout out "Do it myself" and grab the card from the reader's hand. After all the cards have been read, players total their correct predictions (i.e., the number of cards in their hand marked FT and the number of cards grabbed from their hand marked DIM.

9. Declare players in each pair with the most correct predictions winners.

10. Debrief players. Ask players to tell whether they chose DIM or FT more frequently. Have them give their reasons. On a flip chart, list types of learning projects which might be facilitated more effectively via self-directed learning. List other learning projects which might more efficiently be achieved through formal classroom training.

**VARIATION**

Provide players with five cards containing only the DIM and FT boxes. Have them write on each card something they have learned during the past two years and check one of the boxes to indicate in which mode the learning occurred. Have players read their cards to their partners. Each time the partner thinks the learning was done in the self-directed mode she or he is to call out "Did it yourself" and grab the card. As above, each person's score is computed by totaling the number of correct predictions made. The partner with the most correct predictions wins.

**FOR MORE INFORMATION**

Knowles, M. (1984). *The adult learner: A neglected species* (3rd ed.). Houston: Gulf.

72

## Learning Choice Cards

To make a set of Learning Choice Cards, photocopy the following items on card-stock paper and cut them out.

| | |
|---|---|
| Learn a computer conferencing program<br><br>❏ **DIM**<br><br>❏ **FT** | Learn business practices of new client companies in Russia<br><br>❏ **DIM**<br><br>❏ **FT** |
| Learn to use LCD panel for business presentations<br><br>❏ **DIM**<br><br>❏ **FT** | Learn to drive forklift<br><br>❏ **DIM**<br><br>❏ **FT** |

| Learn how to resolve conflicts with coworkers | Learn culture of company where I was just hired |
|---|---|
| ❏ **DIM**<br><br>❏ **FT** | ❏ **DIM**<br><br>❏ **FT** |
| Learn my rights regarding sexual harassment | Learn about employees with disabilities |
| ❏ **DIM**<br><br>❏ **FT** | ❏ **DIM**<br><br>❏ **FT** |

Learn about retirement
planning

❏ **DIM**

❏ **FT**

Learn to spot a potentially
violent employee

❏ **DIM**

❏ **FT**

# DOMAIN

| TOPIC | Three learning domains |
| --- | --- |

Learning objectives or activities can be placed into three categories or domains of learning; the cognitive, the psychomotor, and the affective. The learning of various intellectual skills falls into the cognitive domain. For example, learning to use a new Web publishing program would be in the cognitive domain. The learning of physical movements is in the psychomotor domain, whereas the learning of values or attitudes is in the affective domain. Learning how to roller blade is an example of a psychomotor skill, and learning to appreciate classical music would fall into the affective domain.

**LEARNING OBJECTIVE**

Participants will be able to identify learning strategies appropriate for selected learning domains.

**NUMBER OF PARTICIPANTS**

Any number in groups of three members each

**PLAYING TIME**

15-20 minutes

**REQUIRED MATERIALS**

A deck of Lucky Domain Cards, paper and pencil for each three players, flip chart, and markers

**TO PLAY**

1. Introduce participants to the three learning domains.
2. Go over the learning objective for the game.
3. Have players divide into groups of three players.
4. Provide each group a deck of Lucky Domain Cards and paper and pencils with which to keep score.
5. Explain that the object of this casino-like game is to be the group with the most matches on their pretend slot machine within a three-minute period. A match is achieved when three cards are rolled (placed) faceup on the table from three separate domains (cognitive, psychomotor, and affective).
6. Inform players that each card in their deck contains examples of learning activities in the cognitive, psychomotor, and affective domains.
7. Tell players that the game is played by first shuffling the deck of Lucky Domain Cards. Three

cards are taken from the top of the deck and placed on the table in three columns approximately three inches apart. If the three cards are not from three separate domains, then three additional cards are placed on top of the original three cards and so on. When the three cards are each from a different learning domain, a match is achieved.

8. Explain that every time a match is achieved, each member of a group reads the contents of one of the cards aloud. Only one person can be reading at a time. Afterwards the group awards itself a point and play continues until the facilitator calls "stop." Each time the deck of playing cards is exhausted, the deck is reassembled and reshuffled. During the three minutes of play a group may go through the deck several times.

9. Direct players to shuffle and roll their cards.

10. Three minutes later call "stop."

11. Determine which group(s) has the highest score(s). Declare it (them) the winner(s).

12. Debrief players. Discuss how learning strategies might vary according to the domain in which a particular goal falls. On a flip chart, list learning strategies which might be more appropriate for the cognitive domain. Do the same for the psychomotor and affective domains. Ask participants to give the learning domain in which they believe it is the most difficult to bring about new learning. Have players give learning activities which might be considered "mixed activities" (i.e., activities falling within more than one learning domain).

**VARIATION**

Provide groups with blank Lucky Domain Cards. Have players write in their own learning activities on the appropriate cards. Play the game according to the above directions.

**FOR MORE INFORMATION**

Bloom, B. (Ed.) (1956). *Taxonomy of educational objectives, the classification of educational goals- Handbook 1: Cognitive domain.* New York: David McKay.
Miller, V. (1979). *The Guidebook for International Trainers in Business and Industry.* New York: Van Nostrand Reinhold.

## Lucky Domain Cards

To make one deck of Lucky Domain Cards, duplicate the following items on card-stock paper and cut them out.

**AFFECTIVE**

Six months of international travel has made Jeff open to trying new foods.

**AFFECTIVE**

Having had Sue for a partner for three months, Patrolman Pete is now in favor of female police officers.

**AFFECTIVE**

After comparing the production figures of plants with and without work teams, Marty prefers the use of teams.

**AFFECTIVE**

Though a smoker herself, Greta finds that after a six-week trial of a smoke-free workplace, she is in favor of it.

**AFFECTIVE**

After experiencing the convenience of E-mail, John now sees it as a necessity for his job.

**AFFECTIVE**

At first scoffing at the new company fitness center, Dee and Sara now see its benefits in the mirror and use it regularly.

**COGNITIVE**

Participating in a technology workshop has helped Frank to better troubleshoot problems on the network.

**COGNITIVE**

Following the advice in a popular new book, Marge is better able to evaluate the performance of subordinates she rarely sees.

## COGNITIVE

Listening to a memory improvement cassette has helped executive hostess Mary recall the names of patrons.

## COGNITIVE

Attending an IRS seminar has enabled George to explain major changes in tax laws to his coworkers.

## COGNITIVE

Gloria can tell her husband the benefits available at her workplace after attending the orientation session.

## COGNITIVE

After viewing a supplier's videotape, salesman Fritz can list the many uses of the new "garden whizz" tool.

**PSYCHOMOTOR**

Thanks to the hospital's Backsaver program, Bert can now lift heavy bales of paper in the printshop without feeling pain.

**PSYCHOMOTOR**

Pilot Paula can fly the new jet with expertise after practicing on the flight simulator.

**PSYCHOMOTOR**

After spending her required internship with a master plumber, Sandra can repair almost any water heater.

**PSYCHOMOTOR**

With a little coaching from his supervisor, mechanic Jessie can install an airbag in record time.

**PSYCHOMOTOR**

By following the instructions in the manual, Jill can operate her department's new text scanner.

**PSYCHOMOTOR**

Participating in monthly toastmaster's meetings has enabled Calvin to incorporate body gestures into his presentations.

**Blank Cards**

To make one deck of blank Lucky Domain Cards, duplicate the following items three times on card-stock paper and cut them out.

**AFFECTIVE**

**AFFECTIVE**

COGNITIVE

COGNITIVE

PSYCHOMOTOR

PSYCHOMOTOR

# POWER LEARNER PLAY-OFFS

| | |
|---|---|
| **TOPIC** | Learning leader qualities |

Some companies that have established high priority learning goals (e.g., Bell Atlantic, Kodak) have used "learning leaders" to accomplish those goals. The idea is to put together a team of highly effective trainers who are not professional trainers. This select group is sent throughout the organization to deliver needed training to coworkers. They do this with such flair that they create an insatiable demand for their courses. Care is taken to select learning leaders who possess specific qualities (e.g. the 20 power sources listed in this game). Of less importance is their current job or role in the company.

**LEARNING OBJECTIVE**

Participants will be able to identify the learning leader powers they believe have the greatest leadership potential for them.

**NUMBER OF PARTICIPANTS**   7-24

**PLAYING TIME**   15-20 minutes

**REQUIRED MATERIALS**

Pencils, Potential Power sheets, deck of Power Source Cards, flip chart, and markers

**TO PLAY**

1. Introduce players to the concept of leadership power.
2. Go over the learning objective for the game.
3. Pass out a pencil and a copy of the Potential Power sheet to each player.
4. Go over the directions at the top of the worksheet.
5. Give participants approximately two minutes to check the five sources of power which they believe hold the most promise for their own learning leading effectiveness.
6. Hold up the deck of Power Source Cards so that everyone can see them. Explain that the deck contains cards for the 20 power sources listed on their sheets, including the five power sources they have just checked.

7. Advise players that they are going to be randomly dealt five Power Source Cards. They may be fortunate enough to be dealt some of the same power sources they have just checked on their Potential Power sheets. Furthermore, they will have an opportunity to trade some of the cards they were dealt for cards they were not lucky enough to receive.

8. Inform participants that the goal of the game is to end up with as many of the five Power Source Cards they checked on their Potential Power sheets as possible.

9. Deal five Power Source Cards to each player.

10. Inform players that when you call "Trade," they are to begin trading power cards. They can trade any number of their five cards for cards of their liking. After three minutes of trading they will receive five points for each card matching the power sources checked on their Potential Power sheets. If they collect cards for all five power sources checked on their Potential Power sheets, they will receive an additional 10 points.

11. Call "Trade." Tell players to get out of their seats and start making swaps.

12. Three minutes later call an end to the trading session and ask players to return to their seats.

13. Have players record five points on their Potential Power sheets (column three) for each of their checked power sources for which they now have Power Source Cards.

14. Have them add an additional 10 points if they have collected all of the power sources checked on their Potential Power sheet.

15. Ask players to add up their scores. Declare the person(s) with the most power points the winner(s).

16. Bestow upon the winner(s) the title "Princess or Prince of Power."

17. Debrief players. Have participants give a couple of their strongest learner leading powers. Ask them to explain how these powers can be used to promote personal mastery in a learning organization. On a flip chart, list some of the advantages teams of learning leaders might have over professional trainers in affecting dramatic changes in an organization.

**VARIATION**

A quick version of the game can be played by passing out a Potential Power worksheet to each player. In column two have participants check their five strongest learning leader powers. Have a player come forward and blindly draw 10 cards from a deck of Power Source Cards. Ask each participant to check the drawn powers in column three of their Potential Power worksheet (points). Declare players with the most matching (checked) items in columns two and three the winner (s). The facilitator may also wish to create a unique version of the game using her or his own list of learning leader powers. Debrief the players as you did in the original version of this game.

**FOR MORE INFORMATION**

Kline, P. & Saunders, B. (1993). *Ten steps to a learning organization.* Arlington, VA: Great Ocean Publishers.

## Power Source Cards

To prepare a deck of Power Source Cards, photocopy the following items on card-stock paper and cut them out. For 7 to 12 players, use three sets of cards, and for 13 to 24 players, use six sets of cards.

| | |
|---|---|
| **Accepting of Criticism** | **Analytical** |
| **Articulate** | **Business Understanding** |
| **Confront Controversial Issues** | **Creative** |
| **Deal with Incorrigible People** | **Facilitate Group Discussions** |

| | |
|---|---|
| **Good Listener** | **Knowledge of Learning** |
| **Patient** | **Persuasive** |
| **Process and Apply Research Findings** | **Sense of Humor** |
| **Systems Thinker** | **Think on One's Feet** |

| Tolerate Ambiguity | Value Individual Differences |
|---|---|
| **Willing to Admit Mistakes** | **Willing to Change Opinion** |

# Power Potential

**Directions**: Carefully read the list of learning leader power sources in column one. Consider how much each source of power might contribute to your own learning leader effectiveness. Place a √ in column two beside the five power sources that hold the greatest potential for you. At the end of the card-trading session record five points in column three for each of the √'d power sources for which you were able to secure a Power Source Card. Award yourself 10 bonus points if you have secured all of your selected power sources. Tally your score at the bottom of column three.

| Learning Leader Powers | √ | Points |
|---|---|---|
| 1. Accepting of criticism | _____ | _____ |
| 2. Analytical | _____ | _____ |
| 3. Articulate | _____ | _____ |
| 4. Business understanding | _____ | _____ |
| 5. Confront controversial issues | _____ | _____ |
| 6. Creative | _____ | _____ |
| 7. Deal with incorrigible people | _____ | _____ |
| 8. Facilitate group discussions | _____ | _____ |
| 9. Good listener | _____ | _____ |
| 10. Knowledge of learning | _____ | _____ |
| 11. Patient | _____ | _____ |
| 12. Persuasive | _____ | _____ |
| 13. Process and apply research findings | _____ | _____ |
| 14. Sense of humor | _____ | _____ |
| 15. Systems thinker | _____ | _____ |
| 16. Think on one's feet | _____ | _____ |
| 17. Tolerate ambiguity | _____ | _____ |
| 18. Value individual differences | _____ | _____ |
| 19. Willing to admit mistakes | _____ | _____ |
| 20. Willing to change opinion | _____ | _____ |
| Bonus Points | | _____ |
| Total number of points earned | | _____ |

# REMEMBER THIS

| | |
|---|---|
| **TOPIC** | Mnemonic memory devices |

As employees are faced with the need to remember the names of clients, computer passwords, and budget codes they often invent techniques or tricks for storing such information in their long-term memories. These techniques are often referred to as mnemonic memory devices. For example, a new employee may remember the first names of individuals in her office more easily if she makes an acronym out of the first letter of each person's first name. Three other mnemonic devices are the peg system, verbal elaboration, and mental imagery. These techniques are described in the Mnemonic Memory Device Cards in this game.

**LEARNING OBJECTIVE**

Participants will be able to use a mnemonic memory device to remember things of greatest importance to them.

**NUMBER OF PARTICIPANTS**

Any number of players

**PLAYING TIME**

17-20 minutes

**REQUIRED MATERIALS**

List of Happy Words, set of Mnemonic Memory Device Cards, pencils, sheets of lined paper, flip chart, and markers.

**TO PLAY**

1. Introduce players to the concept of mnemonic memory devices.
2. Go over the learning objective for the game.
3. Give one Mnemonic Memory Device Card to each participant. The three types of cards (i.e., peg system, verbal elaboration, and mental imagery) should be distributed in equal numbers.
4. Briefly explain the memory devices on the cards (i.e., peg system, verbal elaboration, and mental imagery).
5. Inform players that they are going to be given 10 minutes to memorize a list of 10 Happy Words.
6. Advise participants that they are to memorize the Happy Words by using the memory device given on

their card. They are not to use any other memory technique.

7. Present the Happy Words to the players either by means of an overhead transparency or a flip chart.
8. Tell the players to "begin memorizing."
9. After 10 minutes tell the participants to "stop memorizing."
10. Cover up the Happy Words.
11. Pass out pencils and sheets of lined paper to each person.
12. Direct players to write down the list of Happy Words they have just memorized.
13. Redisplay the Happy Words and instruct players to check their lists for accuracy.
14. Ask all players who correctly wrote down all 10 Happy Words to stand. Declare these individuals winners.
15. Debrief players. Ask players if they thought they might use their particular memory device in the near future. Request that they explain why they would or would not use it. On a flip chart, list some of the things participants say they have the most trouble remembering. Beside each item list some techniques players have successfully used to remember such items.

**VARIATION**

Instead of using the list of Happy Words to memorize, ask six people from the audience to come forward. Pin very large name tags to their blouses or shirts. Do not use the peoples' real names. Include a mix of common and unusual names. Tell the players to use the memory device given on their cards and give players five minutes to memorize the names of individuals standing before them. You may also want to substitute memory techniques provided by members of the audience for those listed in this game .

**FOR MORE INFORMATION**

Kelly, E. B. (1994). *Memory Enhancement for Educators.* Bloomington, IN: Phi Delta Kappa Educational Foundation.
Mastropieri, M. A. & Scruggs, T. E. (1991). *Teaching Students Ways to Remember: Strategies for Learning Mnemonically.* Cambridge, MA: Brookline Books.

# Happy Words

1. apple
2. dance
3. hello
4. ovation
5. proud
6. puppy
7. rose
8. smile
9. warm
10. yuletide

## Mnemonic  Memory  Device   Cards

To prepare a set of Mnemonic Memory Device  Cards, photocopy the following items on card-stock paper and cut  them out.

---

### Peg System

| | | | | |
|---|---|---|---|---|
| 1. Bun | 3. Tree | 5. Hive | 7. Heaven | 9. Line |
| 2. Shoe | 4. Door | 6. Sticks | 8. Gate | 10. Hen |

To memorize the ten Happy Words, link each peg word with its corresponding number on the Happy Word list using imagery.
For example: If your first word (#1) is monkey, picture a monkey eating a hot cross bun. If your second (#2) word is flower, perhaps you may picture a shoe with a flower arrangement tucked in it. Continue down the list in this manner.

---

### Verbal Elaboration

In this method use the Happy Words in a rhyme or song.
For example: Using the words book, cash, cook, dog, fast, great, green, smart, sofa, steak, a rhyme might be the following:
There on a green sofa reading a book
Sat a smart dog awaiting his cook.
A steak would taste great, even some hash.
He'd go for some fast food, if he only had cash.

---

### Mental Imagery

This method involves imagining pictures of what you wish to remember (in this case, the happy words). You may use a picture of a single item or a picture(s) with some or all of the items interacting.
For example: For the words pastry, shooting star, tree, you may imagine a picture of your favorite sweet roll, your favorite movie actor with a gun in his or her hand, and a picture of your favorite tree in your backyard, continuing in the same manner down your list of words. In a picture of these words interacting, you may imagine yourself savoring your favorite pastry while watching a star shoot across the sky above a stately oak tree.

# STUDY BUDDIES

**TOPIC**

Learning styles

Learning style refers to an individual's preferred approach to learning (i.e., the way they behave, feel, and process information in various learning situations). For example, some individuals prefer to learn by "concrete" means. Given an option, they might choose to learn through creating a project or participating in a training simulation. Other individuals might opt to learn through "abstract" means (e.g., reading case studies or viewing a play). While people may have a general tendency to learn new things by either concrete or abstract means, in practice they frequently use both. This is primarily due to the fact that concrete practice is often required to learn the new skill (e.g., to swim the backstroke, to fly an airplane).

**LEARNING OBJECTIVE**

Participants will be able to determine their preferred learning styles.

**NUMBER OF PARTICIPANTS**

Any number

**PLAYING TIME**

15-18 minutes

**REQUIRED MATERIALS**

Pencils, Learning Preference Inventory, and a set of Study Buddy Questions

**TO PLAY**

1. Introduce participants to the concept of learning styles. Explain that some individuals prefer to learn new things by more concrete means, while others prefer more abstract methods. Give examples.
2. Go over the learning objective for the game.
3. Select someone from the audience to be the "study buddy suitor" for the game. Have this person come forward and sit on a chair facing the audience.
4. Explain that during the game this person will select a study buddy (i.e., a person with whom she or he would like to learn something) from the remaining participants.

5. Pass out pencils and a copy of the Learning Preference Inventory to all players except the study buddy suitor.

6. Have all of the potential study buddies answer each of the 14 questions by circling either A or B. They do not tally their scores at this time.

7. Have all the participants in the audience stand. Explain that the study buddy suitor wants to find a compatible study partner. Therefore, she or he is only interested in individuals whose answers on the Learning Preference Inventory match hers or his.

8. Starting with question one, begin reading one question at a time from the Learning Preference Inventory. Have the suitor state her or his preference aloud so that all members of the audience can hear.

9. Direct members of the audience to sit down and remain seated if their answer for a given question is different than the one given by the suitor.

10. Continue the questioning until only three players remain standing or until all 14 questions have been read.

11. Ask the players who remain standing to come to the front of the room. Have them stand at right angles to the audience and the suitor. If there are more than three players, have half of them stand to the right and the other half to the left of the audience.

12. Give a copy of the Study Buddy Questions to the suitor.

13. Explain that the suitor will now read two questions to the standing finalists. Each finalist is to answer each question that is asked. The suitor will select a study buddy based on their answers.

14. Have the suitor read, and the finalists answer, two Study Buddy Questions. The suitor can pick out which of the five questions to read. (If there are more than three finalists, direct the suitor to read two questions to the group to left of the audience and select a finalist from that group. Have her or him do the same to the group to the right of the audience. Next have the suitor read the last Study Buddy Question to the remaining two finalists. Once they are eliminated from the competition, have finalists return to their seats.

15. Using responses given by the two finalists, direct the suitor to select a "study buddy."

16. Declare this person the winner.

17. Congratulate the two study buddies.

18. Debrief the audience. Discuss the advantages and disadvantages of having a learning partner or team of learners with similar learning styles. Using the scoring instructions at the bottom of their Learning Preference Inventory, have participants compute their abstract and concrete learning preference scores. Ask players if they think their highest score accurately reflects their general learning preference (i.e., concrete versus abstract). Discuss ways trainers and managers might better accommodate learning style differences among employees.

**VARIATION**

Have participants complete and score the Learning Preferences Inventory. Give participants five minutes to find a study buddy in the room who has responded to eight or more inventory questions with the same answers. Declare these individuals winners. Debrief players as in the original version of this game.

**FOR MORE INFORMATION**

Kolb, D. A., Rubin, I. M., & McIntyre, J. M. (1974). *Organizational psychology: An experiential approach* (2nd ed.). Englewood Cliffs, NJ: Prentice-Hall, Inc.

# Learning Preferences Inventory

**Directions**: Carefully read each question and circle either A or B.

1. In learning how to operate a high-tech copy machine, you would prefer to:
   A. watch a demonstration
   B. read the operator's manual.

2. In learning how to perform as part of a team you would prefer to:
   A. participate in outdoor initiatives.
   B. review case studies.

3. In learning to build your business vocabulary, you would prefer to:
   A. complete word puzzles.
   B. play a video game like Wheel of Fortune.

4. In learning to select the best computer hardware for your needs, you would prefer to:
   A. experiment with different types.
   B. view video tapes from manufacturers.

5. In memorizing the products your company makes, you would prefer to:
   A. write a little poem containing them all.
   B. look at slides of each.

6. In learning to write quarterly reports, you would prefer to:
   A. complete workbook exercises.
   B. learn by writing reports.

7. In learning about your company's history, you would prefer:
   A. seeing a play about the company
   B. creating a showcase on the company's history.

8. In learning to understand your department's budget, you would prefer to:
   A. complete a computer-aided instructional module.
   B. examine graphs of income and expenditures.

9. In learning the names of your company's most valued clients, you would prefer to:
   A. make up word games to recall them.
   B. view pictures of them.

10. In learning new customer service policies, you would prefer to:
    A. play a simulation game.
    B. listen to a lecture.

11. In learning to manage conflict with others, you would prefer to:
    A. listen to audio cassettes.
    B. engage in role plays.

12. In learning about your company's projected sales, you would prefer to:
    A. view them in the form of three-dimensional computer graphics.
    B. study prepared tables.

13. In learning to better understand the culture of foreign clients, you would prefer to:
    A. watch travelogues on television.
    B. take a field trip to selected countries.

14. In learning how to conduct more effective performance appraisals, you would prefer to:
    A. practice conducting them.
    B. discuss them with experienced managers.

## Scoring

To determine your preferred learning style (i.e., abstract vs. concrete), total your "A" answers on odd-numbered questions and "B" answers on even-numbered questions. This is your abstract learning score. Next, total your "B" answers on odd-numbered questions and "A" answers on even-numbered questions. This is your concrete learning score. Your overall preferred learning style is determined by your highest score.

_____ Abstract Learning Score _____ Concrete Learning Score

## Study Buddy Questions

1.  Do you prefer to study with fluorescent light or candlelight?

2.  Would you find it easier to study while drinking hot tea or a cold wine cooler?

3.  Who would you rather have for a workshop facilitator, Fred Rogers or Sam Donaldson?

4.  Where do you think you can get the best education for life, Wall Street or Sesame Street?

5.  Which would you rather learn about, the benefits of using snake-charming methods on your boss or the art of creating messages for your answering machine?

# TEACHING MACHINE

**TOPIC**

Instructional models

There are four general models of instruction: (1)Subject-Centered, (2)Objective-Centered, (3)Experience-Centered, and (4)Opportunity-Centered. The subject-centered model is based on pedagogical principles. Advocates of this model believe that professionally trained instructors should plan instruction. The instruction should be carefully sequenced according to the natural structure of the subject matter to be taught. Learners are expected to acquire a general awareness of the information presented. The model works best with younger learners or individuals who have no prior knowledge of the subject-matter content.

The objective-centered model is based on principles of behavioral psychology. Learning is defined as the acquisition of new behaviors. Such behaviors are modeled, practiced, and continuously reinforced with positive rewards. The objective-centered model is recommended when learners must acquire measurable or observable skills.

The experience-centered instruction model has its theoretical roots in cognitive psychology. Whereas the behaviorists achieve learning through psychological "conditioning," cognitivists attempt to facilitate learning through the development of internal classification schemes in the mind (i.e., cognitive maps). The model is used to promote understanding more than behavioral change. It works best in situations where the aim is to stimulate examination and creativity.

Opportunity-centered instruction is based on principles found in humanistic psychology and adult education (andragogy). The aim is to assist adult learners in directing and being responsible for their own learning. The model works best when the emphasis is on such things as problem solving, personal growth, and career or life planning.

**LEARNING OBJECTIVE**   Participants will be able to match learning outcomes with appropriate instructional models.

**NUMBER OF PARTICIPANTS**   8-24 divided into groups of four players each

**PLAYING TIME**   15-20 minutes

**REQUIRED MATERIALS**   Learning Outcome Cards, envelopes, Role Cards, straight pins, flip chart, and markers

**TO PLAY**

1. Explain to participants the four instructional models (i.e., subjected-centered, objective-centered, experience-centered, and opportunity-centered.
2. Go over the learning objective for the game.
3. Inform participants that they will be divided into groups of four and assume the roles of "instructional chips" of a new high-tech teaching machine. Members of each group will play the roles of subject-centered, objective-centered, experience-centered, and opportunity-centered silicon chips.
4. Divide participants into groups of four and have them occupy different areas around the room.
5. Provide each group a set of Role Cards and straight pins.
6. After players have pinned their Role Cards to their blouses or shirts, have them arrange themselves in the formation of a square. Players should be arranged in such a way that the lower left corner is occupied by Role Card #1 (i.e., subject-centered) and continue numerically clockwise around the square.
7. Tell players that they are parts of a machine that miraculously analyzes any learning outcome that is fed into it and prescribes an appropriate instructional model for achieving that outcome.
8. Advise participants that upon receiving an input (i.e., learning outcome), they are to pass the outcome around the group in a clockwise direction at the speed of 186,000 miles per second. Each time the outcome leaves their hand, they are to make a high-pitched electronic sound. This will signify that the outcome has been electronically scanned and analyzed.
9. Explain that when you call "Output," the outcome envelope is to stop moving around the group. It is to remain in the hands of the person holding the

envelope at the time you call "Output." The person holding the envelope will then read the outcome to the group which must decide if it stopped on the correct chip (i.e., appropriate instructional model). Groups will have 30 seconds to make their decision. Two points will be awarded when the outcome stops on the appropriate chip and the group recognizes it as the appropriate chip. One point will be awarded when the outcome stops on the wrong chip and the group recognizes the correct chip. Otherwise, no points are awarded.

10. Provide each group with a learning outcome to process. All groups should be given the same outcome. After 15 to 45 seconds call "Output."

11. Give each group 30 seconds to determine if their outcome stopped on the correct chip.

12. Ask each group, one at a time, to call out the chip their outcome landed on and whether they believe it to be the correct chip. Record the points earned by each group as you go around the room. Make no mention of the correct chip at this time.

13. Give the correct answer and repeat steps 10 through 12 seven more times.

14. At the end of round eight total each group's points. Declare the group with the most points the winners.

15. Debrief players. On a flip chart, make a three-column diagram large enough so that all can see. In column one, list some of the training that is most frequently provided by participants' employers (e.g., new-employee orientation, sales training, safety training). In column two beside each type of training, list which of the four instructional models is typically used to deliver this training. In column three, list the instructional model participants believe is most appropriate to the respective types of training. Discuss instances on the chart where the instructional model most frequently used (column two) differs from that recommended by players (column three).

**VARIATION**

Have participants create a set of new learning outcomes they would like to effect in their own organization. Using four outcomes of the highest priority, play the game according to the above directions.

**FOR MORE INFORMATION**

Rothwell, W. J., & Scrdl, Henry J. (1992). *The ASTD reference guide to professional human resource*

*development roles & competencies* (Vol. I & II, 2nd ed.).
Amherst, MA: HRD Press.

Answers  #1-Subject-centered, #2-Experience-centered, #3-Objective-centered, #4-Opportunity-centered, #5-Subject-centered, #6-Opportunity-centered, #7-Experience-centered, #8-Objective-centered

## Learning Outcome Cards

To make a set of Learning Outcome Cards, photocopy the following items on card-stock paper and cut them out.

**Outcome #1**

The waitresses at Zippy's Cafe must be able to recite the list of specials of the day to customers.

**Outcome #2**

Computer technicians at Acme Technology must be able to diagnose the source of software conflicts.

**Outcome #3**

Drivers at Miller's disposal must be able to properly empty dumpsters into their trucks.

**Outcome #4**

Employees at Shysters Investment Brokers are encouraged to pursue educational opportunities outside their areas of technical expertise.

**Outcome #5**

By the end of the second class, all safety trainers must know the first and last names of participants.

**Outcome #6**

Employees at Starburst Publishing must have a complete and up-to-date career plan.

**Outcome #7**

Claims processors at Happy Valley Insurance must be able to apply the provisions in each type of life insurance policy.

**Outcome #8**

The foremen at Wilson's Tool and Die must be able to make simple repairs to all drill presses.

## Role Cards

To make a set of Role Cards, photocopy the following items on card-stock paper and cut them out.

| | |
|---|---|
| **Subject-Centered** | **Objective-Centered** |
| **Experience-Centered** | **Opportunity-Centered** |

## TOP THIS

| TOPIC | Learning hierarchy |
|---|---|

Learning objectives and activities can be classified according to learning domains (see the game "Domain"). They can also be placed in hierarchies ranging from the simple to the complex. Complex learning is often referred to as "higher-order learning." Simpler learning is sometimes referred to as "lower-order learning." Lower-order learning in a particular field is followed by higher-order learning. The cognitive domain includes a hierarchy of intellectual skills: knowledge, comprehension, application, analysis, synthesis, and evaluation.

The most basic intellectual skill is that of possessing knowledge or knowing certain information (e.g., products or services your company provides). A slightly more advanced intellectual skill is that of comprehension. Comprehension involves being able to understand and explain a concept (e.g., explaining a clause in a warranty agreement). The next intellectual level is application. Application is being able to put to use what has been learned (e.g., adhering to practices learned in safety training, a machinist operates his lathe safely). Analysis refers to breaking down material into its component parts and/or relationships (e.g., identifying the informal structures of a company). The opposite of analysis is synthesis, (i.e., the combining of material to form an integrated whole). An example of synthesis is the reorganization or restructuring of a company. The highest or most complex cognitive skill is that of evaluation. Evaluation entails the judging of persons, things, or processes based on selected criteria (e.g., determining which companies should receive the Malcolm Baldridge Award).

**LEARNING OBJECTIVE**

Participants will be able to determine the level of learning activities and adjust their learning strategies accordingly.

**NUMBER OF PARTICIPANTS**

Any even number in pairs

**PLAYING TIME**

7-12 minutes

**REQUIRED MATERIALS**   A deck of Top This Cards for each pair of players

**TO PLAY**

1. Introduce participants to the concept of higher- and lower-order learning activities.
2. Go over the learning objective for the game.
3. Divide participants into pairs.
4. Provide each pair with a deck of Top This Cards. Hand the deck to the person in each pair whose last name comes first alphabetically (e.g., Jones comes before Smith. Jones gets the cards and deals first).
5. Explain that the object of the game is to collect the largest number of tricks during two rounds of play.
6. Advise participants that the game begins with the dealer thoroughly shuffling the deck and dealing nine cards each to his partner and herself or himself.
7. Tell players that the dealer's opponent reads and lays down the first card. As cards are laid down players are to call out "Top this!" The dealer follows by reading and laying down a card containing a higher number. Each card contains a number signifying the level of complexity of the stated learning activity. Each player attempts to secure the trick by reading and laying down a card with a higher number. The player who lays down the highest numbered card gets to collect the trick. After collecting their trick, a player must read and lay down a card with their partner attempting to top it.
8. Inform participants that a round of play ends when the players run out of cards. After recording a point for each trick picked up, the cards are reshuffled and the next round of play begins.
9. Direct players to begin two rounds of play.
10. After all of the pairs have played two rounds, have the player(s) with the highest score stand. Declare them winners.
11. Debrief players. Have participants discuss the type of learning activities they are most frequently engaged in--lower-versus higher-order. Have them list some challenges and rewards for engaging in the higher-order activities. Get their opinions on whether they believe the frequency of higher-order learning activities have increased for them over the past five years. If so, ask them to elaborate on why the increase has occurred.

| | |
|---|---|
| **VARIATION** | Provide groups with blank Top This Cards. Have players write in their own learning activities on the appropriate cards. Play the game according to the above directions. |
| **FOR MORE INFORMATION** | Bloom, B. (Ed.) (1956). *Taxonomy of educational objectives, the classification of educational goals-Handbook 1: Cognitive domain.* New York: David McKay. Miller, V. (1979). *The guidebook for international trainers in business and industry.* New York: Van Nostrand Reinhold. |

# Top This Cards

To make one deck of Top This Cards, duplicate the following items on card-stock paper and cut them out.

| | |
|---|---|
| **Knowledge**<br><br>**1**<br><br>Laura advised the caller of the store's hours. | **Knowledge**<br><br>**1**<br><br>Melvin quoted the company's mission in his speech. |
| **Knowledge**<br><br>**1**<br><br>Betty told Jerry the sales department's extension number. | **Comprehension**<br><br>**2**<br><br>Lana paraphrased the boss's instructions to her coworkers. |

**Comprehension**

**2**

Richard explained the profit sharing plan to the new employee.

**Comprehension**

**2**

Steve spelled out the company's new sexual harassment policy.

**Application**

**3**

In dismissing Mr. Branch, the supervisor closely followed her company's guidelines.

**Application**

**3**

Prior to painting the shop floor, Phil properly prepared the surface.

**Application**

**3**

In making her request for additional travel money, Margaret followed company protocol.

**Analysis**

**4**

Harry identified the source of recent leaks of information to the press.

**Analysis**

# 4

Chuck located the cause of frequent shutdowns in the computer network.

**Analysis**

# 4

Lei Chu ascertained the company's most profitable product lines.

**Synthesis**

# 5

Nancy designed a highly innovative mentoring program for her division.

**Synthesis**

# 5

Larry created a home page on the Internet for his business.

**Synthesis**

# 5

Maria organized an Asian food exposition in her city.

**Evaluation**

# 6

Faye evaluated John's performance according to departmental standards.

| Evaluation | Evaluation |
|---|---|
| **6** | **6** |
| Zeke field-tested the company's new product. | The Board carefully considered the buyout offer. |

## Blank Top This Cards

To make one deck of blank Top This Cards, duplicate the following items on card-stock paper and cut them out.

| Knowledge | Knowledge |
|---|---|
| **1** | **1** |

| Knowledge | Comprehension |
|:---:|:---:|
| 1 | 2 |

| Comprehension | Comprehension |
|:---:|:---:|
| 2 | 2 |

| Application | Application |
|:---:|:---:|
| 3 | 3 |

| | |
|---|---|
| **Application**<br><br>3 | **Analysis**<br><br>4 |
| **Analysis**<br><br>4 | **Analysis**<br><br>4 |
| **Synthesis**<br><br>5 | **Synthesis**<br><br>5 |

**Synthesis**

5

**Evaluation**

6

**Evaluation**

6

**Evaluation**

6

# Chapter Four

# Remodeling Games

# BEWITCHING BEHAVIORS

**TOPIC**    Superstitions as cultural mindsets

Superstitions are commonly held beliefs and practices associated with the unknown or with supernatural forces. They can be a part of the cultural belief system of a country or a company. In the United States there are more than a million superstitions affecting how people behave. Many of these superstitions constitute a mental model whereby a certain behavior is thought to produce a specified result (e.g., knocking on wood wards off bad luck). The cause-and-effect relationship seldom has any basis in modern science. However, the belief continues to be passed on from one generation to the next.

**LEARNING
OBJECTIVE**    Participants will be able to identify superstitious mindsets found in their own organizations

**NUMBER OF
PARTICIPANTS**    8 to 40 players

**PLAYING TIME**    10-15 minutes depending upon the number of players

**REQUIRED
MATERIALS**    Set of Superstition Cards

**TO PLAY**
1. Introduce players to the concept of superstitions as cultural and company mindsets (i.e., mental models).
2. Go over the learning objective for the game.
3. Explain that they are about to be handed a card which constitutes one part of a superstition. One person in the room will receive the "cause" portion of the superstition and another person will receive the "effect" or "result" part of the superstition. All cause cards will contain the number "2" and all effects cards will contain the number " 1."
4. Inform participants that they are to find the other person in the room holding the second half of their superstition.
5. Tell players that they will have three to six minutes (three minutes for groups with 10 or fewer members and six minutes for groups with 11 or more members) to find the other half of their superstition. Once they have located the other half

of their superstition, the two players are to stand together until the end of game.

6. Shuffle Superstition Cards in front of players. Make certain the stack contains a correct number of matching cause-and-effect cards. Request that a participant come forward and cut the deck.

7. Go around the room having each participant draw one card from the top of the stack.

8. Give players the appropriate amount of time (three or six minutes) to locate the other half of their superstition.

9. After three or six minutes call "Time."

10. Have players read their superstitions aloud, first the cause and then the effect. Congratulate players with correct matches.

11. Debrief players. Have players give some superstitions that were passed on to them by their parents. Ask them to share some superstitions that still influence their behavior (e.g., refuse to walk under ladders or step on cracks). List, on a flip chart, superstitions currently held by employees within their own company. Discuss superstitions that may be having a negative impact on the participants' company, how such superstitions might have originated, and how they should be handled.

**VARIATION**

Play the game using superstition cards made up by employees in the company. The result or effect cards might include such things as "to get a raise," "to get a promotion," "to get into the in crowd," "to get fired," or "to get into the company newsletter." Remind players that to be a real superstition there should be no actual or known relationship between the causes and the effects appearing on the cards. However, there should be some belief on the part of employees that the superstition just might be true.

**FOR MORE INFORMATION**

Sarnoff, J. & Ruffins, R. (1980). *If you were really superstitious.* New York: Charles Scribner's Sons. Schwartz, A. (Ed.), & Rounds, G. (Illus.) (1974). *Cross your fingers, spit in your hat.* New York: J. B. Lippincott Company.

Answers

1. To keep a bridegroom faithful,

   2. preserve part of the wedding cake.

1. To get more milk from your cows,

   2. have a woman milk them.

1. To win the love of another,

   2. feed her or him tomatoes.

1. To make a dream come true,

   2. tell it before breakfast.

1. To keep from catching cold all winter,

   2. catch a falling leaf on the first day of autumn.

1. To do well on a test,

   2. use the same pencil to take it that you used in studying.

1. To hit well in a baseball game

   2. always spit on your hands before picking up the bat.

1. To win over your enemies,

   2. kill the first wasp you see each year.

1. To keep bees from stinging you,

   2. hold your breath while one is near.

1. To make sure your money isn't stolen,

   2. wash it in rainwater.

1. To disguise herself from evil spirits,

   2. the bride should wear a veil.

1. To turn your bad luck into good luck,

   2. turn your hat around and pull out your pockets.

1. To cure a cold,

   2. kiss a mule on the nose.

1. To get rid of freckles,

   2. wash your face in buttermilk.

1. To cure hiccups,

   2. bring your little fingers together as close as you can without having them touch.

Answers Continued

1. To find out what your dog dreams about,

2. sleep on the same pillow he uses.

1. To get the best luck from a four-leaf clover,

2. wear it inside your shoe.

1. To avoid sickness in the family,

2. don't pay the doctor in full.

1. To prevent bed sores,

2. put an ax under the bed.

1. To get a good husband,

2. a woman must be able to kindle a good fire.

## Superstition Cards

To prepare a deck of Superstition Cards, make a photocopy of the following items on card-stock paper. Cut out individual cards.

| 1 | 2 |
|---|---|
| To keep a bridegroom faithful, | preserve part of the wedding cake. |

| 1 | 2 |
|---|---|
| To get more milk from your cows, | have a woman milk them. |

| 1 | 2 |
|---|---|
| To win the love of another, | feed her or him tomatoes. |

| | |
|---|---|
| **1**<br><br>To make a dream come true, | **2**<br><br>tell it before breakfast. |
| **1**<br><br>To keep from catching cold all winter, | **2**<br><br>catch a falling leaf on the first day of autumn. |
| **1**<br><br>To do well on a test, | **2**<br><br>use the same pencil to take it that you used in studying. |
| **1**<br><br>To hit well in a baseball game | **2**<br><br>always spit on your hands before picking up the bat. |

| 1 | 2 |
|---|---|
| To win over your enemies, | kill the first wasp you see each year. |
| To keep bees from stinging you, | hold your breath while one is near. |
| To make sure your money isn't stolen, | wash it in rainwater. |
| To disguise herself from evil spirits, | the bride should wear a veil. |

| 1 | 2 |
|---|---|
| To turn your bad luck into good luck, | turn your hat around and pull out your pockets. |
| To cure a cold, | kiss a mule on the nose. |
| To get rid of freckles, | wash your face in buttermilk. |
| To cure hiccups, | bring your little fingers together as close as you can without having them touch. |

| 1 | 2 |
|---|---|
| To find out what your dog dreams about, | sleep on the same pillow he uses. |
| 1 | 2 |
| To get the best luck from a four-leaf clover, | wear it inside your shoe. |
| 1 | 2 |
| To avoid sickness in the family, | don't pay the doctor in full. |
| 1 | 2 |
| To prevent bed sores, | put an ax under the bed. |

| 1 | 2 |
|---|---|
| To get a good husband, | a woman must be able to kindle a good fire. |

# DIVERSITY SCREEN

**TOPIC**

Stereotyping

Stereotypes are mental images people hold in their minds about individuals belonging to a particular group. It is assumed that because members of the group share one distinguishing characteristic (e.g., race, gender, physical condition) they also share a host of other things in common. These are some oversimplified, prejudiced comments: "all Latinos are hot lovers," "men make better chefs," and "blind people have better hearing." The stereotypes employees hold in their heads may cause them to prejudge (i.e., make assumptions about a person without actually knowing the person) new clients, job applicants, and other company employees. Such prejudgments are almost always inaccurate. Furthermore, when such prejudgments are acted upon they can lead to decisions which are not in the best interest of the company.

**LEARNING OBJECTIVE**

Participants will be able to identify some of the harmful effects stereotyping can have on an organization.

**NUMBER OF PARTICIPANTS**

Any number divided into groups of five to seven players

**PLAYING TIME**

15-25 minutes, depending upon the number of players

**REQUIRED MATERIALS**

One die, deck of Diversity Cards, and a deck of Applicant Cards for each small group of players, a flip chart, and markers

**TO PLAY**

1. Introduce players to the concept of stereotyping.
2. Go over the learning objective for the game.
3. Explain to players that they are about to play a game in which they are to be the first in their group to fill three sales positions (i.e., VP for Sales, Sales Manager, and Senior Salesperson).
4. Advise participants that they are to attempt to hire a qualified person for each of the sales positions. However, they are not to hire someone who exhibits the personality or the physical, religious, or cultural characteristics described on their Diversity Card(s).

5. Divide the larger group into small groups of five to seven players each.
6. Pass out a die, deck of Diversity Cards, and deck of Applicant Cards to each group.
7. Ask two people in each group to thoroughly shuffle the cards and place the decks facedown in the middle of the group.
8. Have each of the members in the groups roll the die and draw one to three Diversity Cards from the diversity pile. Tell players that if they roll a 1 or 2, they are to draw one card; if they role a 3 or 4, to draw two cards; and if they roll 5 or 6, they must draw three Diversity Cards.
9. Direct the members of each group to read their Diversity Cards aloud to the other members of their group.
10. Explain that the competition begins with the person in each group who drew the most Diversity Cards drawing the first Applicant Card. The player should read the card aloud to her or his group. If the applicant is qualified for any of the three sales positions (i.e., VP for Sales, Sales Manager, and Senior Salesperson) and does not exhibit any of the characteristics noted on her or his Diversity Cards, the player can keep the Applicant Card. This signifies the hiring of the applicant. If the individual on the drawn Applicant Card is not qualified for any of the available positions or exhibits one or more of the characteristics noted on the players' Diversity Cards, the Applicant Card is returned to the bottom of the Applicant Card pile.
11. Advise participants that after a player has either kept or returned an Applicant Card, play continues in a clockwise direction around the group until a player has successfully filled all three sales positions.
12. Have groups continue to play until each group has a winner.
13. Ask the winners in each of the groups to stand and be recognized.
14. Debrief players. Ask participants to discuss the extent to which they believe various stereotypes positively or negatively affect hiring and promotion practices at their organization. List on a flip chart selected slogans the company uses to sell its products, services, or image. Have players identify and discuss any stereotyping found in the slogans. Request that players write down on a sheet of paper a characteristic by which they might personally be

stereotyped and wrongfully prejudged by strangers (e.g., Catholic, Southerner, athletic appearance). Below the distinguishing characteristic ask players to list at least three ways they differ from the associated stereotype. Share results with others. Solicit ways of testing and holding in check various stereotypes.

**VARIATION**      Play the game using participant-made diversity cards. Have players create their own set of diversity cards based on real employees in their company. Make certain that any information that might reveal the identify of a worker (e.g., real name, position, department) is fictionalized.

**FOR MORE**
**INFORMATION**      Simons, G. & Zuckerman, A. (1995). *Working together: Succeeding in a multicultural organization* (rev. ed.). Menlo Park, CA: Crisp Publications, Inc.

# Diversity Cards

To prepare one deck of Diversity Cards, photocopy the following items on card-stock paper and cut them out.

---

You attended a previously all-white high school which was forced into accepting black students bused in from ghetto schools. Many of the white students, including you, blamed the resulting discord on the attitudes of black students, whom you labeled as troublemakers.

---

In a previous job, you and another person were the only two black employees. Your boss, a white man, gave all the best clients to white or Asian employees who you felt didn't work as hard as you. You think that other races look down on black people and do not judge them to be as competent.

---

When you were growing up, your father and all the males in your family circle were seen as the kings of their castles. Men were more worldly and therefore wiser than women, so females should follow the dictates of men. Women who did not do so were considered hussies or worse.

---

You were raised by a single mother who struggled to survive in a workplace dominated by men. You came to believe that men would almost always discriminate against a woman no matter how intelligent the woman.

132

The working-class family that lived in your neighborhood when you were a child was a rough lot. The father didn't work much, drank a lot, was mean to his family, and turned their property into a junkyard, with cars on blocks and trash all over. You can't see why these people are called "working class", because in your experience, they don't.

Your parents worked many years for a company owned by an upper-class family in town who added to their wealth through the hard work and creative ideas of their underpaid employees. During recessions, the employees had to sacrifice while family members were hired at much higher wages. You see the upper-class as an opportunistic, lazy group.

As an agnostic, you feel that religious beliefs are a very personal matter. You see people who espouse their religion and/or try to persuade others to think the same way as obnoxious and unpleasant to be around.

Your parents were conservative religious people. They taught you that those who do not believe in the literal word of the Christian Bible are heathens who cannot be trusted no matter how pleasant they may seem because they don't have good moral values.

As a kid, your favorite television shows and movies portrayed Italian people as, at the least, criminals if not masterminds of organized crime. Today even an Italian sounding name brings to mind "The Godfather," and you still believe most Italians can't be trusted.

The firm you and several members of your family worked for was bought out by a Japanese company. All of you lost your jobs through the merger. You see this as another example of the Japanese out to make money in your country by putting Americans out of work.

You grew up in a fitness conscious family where only healthy food was eaten and sports and exercise were top priorities. Your parents stressed the fact that lack of physical fitness was a sign that a person lacks the self-discipline necessary to be productive and succeed.

You are a plain-looking person who has lived in the shadow of more attractive people all your life. You feel that even though a plain person like you may be just as qualified or even more qualified for a job, an attractive person has always seemed to have the edge, and you resent it.

During your school years, your parents and teachers repeatedly told you to speak proper English or people would see you as stupid. Today you consider poor grammar as a sign of ignorance.

Friends of your parents had a child who stuttered badly, and you would grow impatient with him when you played together. Your parents told you that he couldn't help stuttering because it was caused by a problem in his brain. Even as an adult, any speech impediment is seen by you as a sign of mental deficiency.

Your best friend was paralyzed from the waist down in a bicycle accident and was confined to a wheelchair. His difficult adjustment, coupled with his not being able to run and play with you as he previously had, has left you with the feeling that handicapped people are limited in their abilities.

Your uncle lost a hand in an industrial accident many years ago. Since that time, he has refused to work at all and uses his disability as an excuse for not doing so. You suspect that handicapped people are inclined to use their disabilities as an excuse for not doing what they don't wish to do.

As a teenager, you worked in a retail business which employed people of various ages. The middle-aged and older people tended to disparage the suggestions and admonish the behavior of the younger employees. You feel that older workers are set in their thinking and are prejudiced against younger people.

A couple of years ago, you hired two young people just out of college. Both of these people seemed to come to work just to collect a paycheck, and they displayed no loyalty to the company. You feel that young people think the world owes them a living.

When you were eight, your beloved grandmother died and a year later your grandfather married a very overbearing woman. She made everyone in the family so uncomfortable that once loved family gatherings became ordeals. Though she's been dead for many years, even slightly pushy people are a turnoff to you.

During the early part of your life, you were surrounded by people with large egos, who made you feel insignificant. You had great difficulty in developing self-confidence and even as an adult, egotistical people make you feel defensive.

Your house has been burglarized twice and you were once mugged on a business trip. Though the others were never caught, one burglar was arrested and sent to jail. After being released, he went back to crime, and you are convinced that criminals cannot be rehabilitated.

# Applicant Cards

To prepare one deck of Applicant Cards, photocopy two copies of the following items on card-stock paper and cut them out.

George Brady is a 51-year-old man who wears a leg brace as a result of polio in childhood. Though he walks with a halting gait, his selling ability won him "Salesperson of the Year" 6 of the 11 years he was with Coca Cola.

Rosie Cappini is a little Italian woman who looks and acts like everybody's mother. She formerly worked for K-Mart as assistant sales manager.

John Goldberg is a young Jewish man born in the Bronx. He has a degree with honors in marketing and his pleasant personality made him very successful in his sales job with Apple Computer for the past four years

Bernice Thompson is a very plump middle-aged woman with a super personality. In her 12-year stay with Hallmark Cards, she worked her way up from salesperson to a top account executive.

Monty Brown has worked hard to overcome his past. He studied and received a bachelor's degree while in prison and later worked five years for Mars Candy Company where his sales volume grew substantially each year.

Jean Patterson is a beautiful woman with bad grammar, developed while growing up in a poor environment. She's a quick learner who believes that a salesperson should know all there is to know about the product line, as evidenced by her spectacular sales record with Avon and later Revlon.

Scott Lawson is one of those lucky people born with stunning good looks and high intelligence into an upper-class family. He has been a sales manager with Kimberly Clark and is looking for new experiences.

Linda Jones is an aggressive woman with an attitude that reflects her strong feminist beliefs. She relates very well to women which may account for her great success with Clairol.

Carol Warner is a competent woman with a cheerful outlook who endears herself to most people. Overcoming shyness caused by a pronounced stutter, she has been a top salesperson at J.C. Penney for over eight years.

Freddie Mills, a black man from a working class background, has worked hard, putting himself through college, graduating at 33. Now six years later, he has several sales awards for superior performance at Hasbro Toys.

At 53, Howard Morgan projects himself as a man's man, viewing women as sweet little things, but not as capable as men. At present, he is a sales manager for Firestone Tires.

People say that Tony Risotti looks a bit like a Mafia hitman although he's a gentleman of high integrity and intelligence. His charm and sincerity has instilled customer confidence as his sales record in electronics at Sears indicates.

June Li is a 45-year-old woman of Japanese birth. Her outgoing positive demeanor made her a successful and popular salesperson at Sara Lee.

Russ Anderson, a working-class white man, admits to being a bit uncomfortable working with other races. He has a history of hard work, several years of experience, and outstanding customer rapport during his years as assistant sales manager at a Jewel Food store.

Lewis Pearce, a man of working-class speech and values, has been a sales leader with Seagrams for the past 16 years. Now at 50, he is looking for a supervisory opportunity.

Sylvia Long has an impressive track record in sales for both Kimberly Clark and Birdseye Foods. Now after 18 months in prison on drug charges, her rehabilitation has resulted in a strong Buddhist faith.

Sam Chin has a record of million-dollar sales awards for the past three years at IBM. Two years of his work with the company was done in his native Japan.

Buffy Highfield is a small attractive upper-class woman just three years out of college. A 4.0 grade point average in her marketing courses was a promising start to her next three years of outstanding sales at her grandfather's distributing company.

Jim Little, a man of rugged good looks and a charming manner, is well aware of his appeal and is very condescending to coworkers and those he believes beneath him. This character trait may have been what kept him from advancing up the sales management ladder with Microsoft.

Maggie Cantrell, an outspoken woman with a pushy disposition, seems to be able to turn her charm on or off at will. Though her former boss and coworkers at Rhodes Furniture found her abrasive, they are quick to praise her excellent sales abilities.

Ben Maxwell lost his left arm during the Vietnam conflict. His sterling sales record with 3M since his military discharge has not been affected by this unfortunate circumstance.

Mario Minelli had a six-figure annual sales record with Eaton Corporation for the past five years until cutbacks caused his layoff. A rocky start in the working-class section of Boston and a teenage arrest for theft are far in the past for Mario.

Harvey Field is a 52-year-old black man with 30 years of sales experience. He has sold eight different product lines in his career with his last position being at Montgomery Ward in the automotive department.

Abigail Feinberg is an aggressive 32-year-old Jewish woman who has been active in women's issues. This interest in women's problems has aided in making her a sales leader with Johnson and Johnson.

Jessica Carson is a stunning upper-class woman with an advanced degree in marketing. In her four years with Maytag, she has demonstrated superior sales ability.

Gary McDowell is a 23-year-old man with one year of full-time and four years of part-time sales experience. In spite of speech filled with a great deal of slang and less than perfect grammar, he has excellent rapport with the young set as evidenced by his outstanding sales for Radio Shack.

Maria Lopez is a middle-aged woman of strong Catholic beliefs. Her unassuming attitude has resulted in remarkable sales at a local electric supply firm, often selling to men who behaved chivalrously to the little lady.

Russell Jensen is a 50ish very plump good natured man who is well liked by everyone he meets. After almost 25 years of excellent sales with Metropolitan Insurance, he wishes to slow down a bit and try something new.

Caroline White is an egotistical woman who has a tendency to denigrate the efforts of her peers. She is extremely proud of her tenure as sales manager at Macy's, but feels that her talents may be more valuable elsewhere.

Ahmal Hussein, a devout follower of Islam, is a very capable and amiable man. Since coming to the United States 12 years ago, he has worked his way up in the sales department at the local store of a lumber company chain.

Alex Warren has been a top salesperson for Ace Hardware for the last 10 years, winning several awards. Silver-haired at 48, he is an attractive man with a slightly stiff walk, the result of a skiing accident as a teen.

Cathy Nolan is an attractive young lady who is a native of New York City, as her very pronounced accent indicates. Her outgoing personality has helped her become an outstanding sales person for the Jewel Box.

Ramona Nickelby is a short chubby woman whose dress and outlook reflect her devotion to the metaphysical. She says using her ESP in relating to the needs of customers is responsible for her successful sales career at Southern Bell Telephone.

Al Harris, a 55-year old-man with a pudgy middle, has a slight limp from an old gunshot wound he sustained in breaking into a service station as a teen. Since that time, he has become a very successful salesperson for Scott Paper.

Bill Golonka is a tall, fit, attractive man who is at times quite overbearing, especially to women. He has been supervisor of the sales force of a small town newspaper.

Scott Bergman is a balding, round man who, besides being a superb salesperson at Random House books, is an active board member at his Unitarian Church. His open and accepting manner has helped him reach his high sales goals each year.

Lizzie Carlson is an upbeat black woman with a ready laugh and sparkling wit. In the past 10 years with Target Stores, she has won 12 sales awards.

Phil Martin was a sales manager with Alcoa for eight years until downsizing cut his job and then for five years with Cablevision. He received praise from the majority of his subordinates. In spite of the loss of a hand in an accident, he has a stellar career record.

Rick Petrillo is a handsome man with remarkable sales ability. Multimillion dollar sales of automobiles at a BMW dealership are an impressive part of his resume.

Frank Watts was born to Hindu parents in a working-class section of Los Angeles. Being black himself, his rapport with black people in his sales area has enabled him to build an impressive sales record in that community.

142

Carla Phillips is one tough lady who has worked hard developing a winning sales technique at Sportmart. An aggressive personality overshadows poor grammar and a slight stutter.

Sarah Goldberg is a 56-year-old woman who enthusiastically devotes herself to selling her products, only taking time off to celebrate the Jewish sabbath and holidays. A talkative and motherly approach to her customers earns her a comfortable income working for Sterling Drugs.

Lisa Feldon is a tall, beautiful woman who knows how to use her physical attributes to their best advantage in her sales job at Cover Girl Cosmetics. She has outsold all her fellow salespeople for the past two years.

Maurice Swanson supervised a multimillion dollar sales force at B. F. Goodrich. At 49, with a six-month prison stay for income tax evasion behind him, he wants to use his years of experience to build a thriving sales record.

Bob Davis lost his lower left leg in a military air crash. After being discharged from the Air Force, he began selling products for Colgate Palmolive and now is a top salesman at Office Depot.

Leslie Jordan, is an upper-class lady whose family fell on hard times. She was forced to embark on a sales career that after 10 years, reflects a natural sales ability. She has done so well with Zenith Electronics that she is again driving a sleek sports car.

John Berman graduated 20 years ago from a private Mormon college with an MBA. He has been a sales manager for Allstate Insurance for the past 10 years. In his years before retirement he wants to build a new career in a different type of sales.

Marshall Denby is a 35-year-old black man who grew up in a housing development on the near south side of Chicago. With a business degree and 10 years of outstanding sales performance at Mobil Oil, the only hint of his former life is an occasional slip in grammar.

Conrad Liston is an imperious man of upper-class lineage and portly girth. His ability to wheel and deal with management has provided him a very comfortable living selling for General Mills.

Mary Fishburn is a 30-year-old black woman who's a bit on the domineering side. For three years she worked for a Toyota dealership, breaking the company sales record in her first year.

# GAP GAPERS FEUD

**TOPIC**  Delta analysis

Gap analysis, also known as delta analysis, is a means of identifying the difference between two states (e.g., the way things are now and the way someone would like them to be). The process can also be used to compare differences between what is said to be the case and the actual situation. Gap analysis is frequently part of a company's attempt to systematically plan the needed steps to move it from "how things are now" to "how they would like things to be in the future."

**LEARNING OBJECTIVE**  Participants will be able to perform a gap analysis of a company's public image.

**NUMBER OF PARTICIPANTS**  Any number of players

**PLAYING TIME**  8-12 minutes depending upon the number of players

**REQUIRED MATERIALS**  Pencils, Gap Gapers Worksheet

**TO PLAY**
1. Introduce participants to the gap analysis approach to analyzing mindsets promoted by companies through slogans and advertising.
2. Go over the learning objective for the game.
3. Explain to players that they will be given a Gap Gapers Worksheet containing the names of 10 companies along with their well-known mindsets. Tell participants that they will be asked to rate the accuracy of the public images based upon their own perceptions of truth.
4. Inform players that as in the popular television game show *Family Feud*, an identical survey has been given to a group of college business students. The winner of the game will be the person(s) in the room whose answers most closely correspond to the ratings of the students.
5. Pass out game materials to each player.
6. After going over the directions on the worksheet, have players rate the respective 10 items.
7. Give players the results of the survey. Have them underline the mean rating for each of the 10 items.

8. To compute their scores, ask players to calculate the numerical difference between their rating and that of the survey (circled versus underlined numbers) for each of the 10 items on the worksheet. Each difference should be written in the left margin next to the name of each company.

9. Have participants total their individual item differences and record it in the upper-right-hand corner of their worksheets. Declare the player(s) with the lowest score(s) the winner(s).

10. Debrief players. Ask players to list companies which they and the survey participants both found highly credible. Discuss why these companies appear to have such a small credibility gap (difference between the promoted and the publicly perceived image of the company). Have players list companies which they and survey participants both found to have large credibility gaps. See if players think large credibility gaps are due to dishonesty on the part of companies, the inability or unwillingness of some companies to see things as they really are, or an effort on the part of companies to get employees to live up to what the company hopes will be a self-fulfilling prophecy.

**VARIATION**     Play the game using selected departments in a given company. Before playing the game, have departments submit a mindset they would like others to believe about their unit. Survey managers in the company to determine their perceived accuracy of the mindsets. Compare results of the managers' survey to those playing the game. Participants' ratings might also be compared to those of customers.

**FOR MORE
INFORMATION**     Moskowitz, M., Levering, R., & Katz, M. (Eds.) (1990). *Everybody's business: A field guide to 400 leading companies in America.* New York: Currency/Doubleday.

Answers

Answers most frequently given by a survey group consisting of graduate students in management and human resource development:

| 1. | 3 | 5. | 3 | 9. | 3 |
| 2. | 2 | 6. | 2 | 10. | 2 |
| 3. | 4 | 7. | 3 | | |
| 4. | 3 | 8. | 4 | | |

# GAP GAPERS WORKSHEET

**Directions:** Listed below are 10 companies along with the mindsets they would like you to believe about the organization. Using the following scale, circle the number below each company that best corresponds to your perceived accuracy of the stated mindset.

| FALSE | MOSTLY FALSE | SOMEWHAT TRUE | MOSTLY TRUE | TRUE |
|---|---|---|---|---|
| 0 | 1 | 2 | 3 | 4 |

1. **FORD** - At Ford, Quality is Job #1

0   1   2   3   4

2. **DELTA AIRLINES** - At Delta we love to fly and it shows

0   1   2   3   4

3. **UPS** - We run the tightest ship in the shipping business

0   1   2   3   4

4. **LENSCRAFTERS** - Eyeglasses in about an hour

0   1   2   3   4

5. **WALMART** - The home of falling prices

0   1   2   3   4

6. **SHARP** - From sharp minds come Sharp products

0   1   2   3   4

7. **STOUFFERS** - Nothing comes closer to home

0   1   2   3   4

8. **HALLMARK CARDS** - When you care to send the very best

0   1   2   3   4

9. **ANHEUSER-BUSCH** - Budweiser, the king of beers

0   1   2   3   4

10. **BURGER KING** - Have it your way at Burger King

0   1   2   3   4

# Great Siberian Freeze Off

| | |
|---|---|
| **TOPIC** | Unfreezing and refreezing |

Kurt Lewin's Change Model proposes that group learning takes place through a three-phase process of unfreezing old beliefs, the restructuring of those beliefs, and the refreezing or acceptance of new beliefs. According to the model, old beliefs and habits that interfere with new learning are best unfrozen through conscious intentions and the anticipation of potential benefits. New learning is best refrozen through repeated opportunities to practice the new beliefs and habits.

**LEARNING OBJECTIVE**

Participants will be able to use Kurt Lewin's Change Model to effect changes in employees' mindsets.

**NUMBER OF PARTICIPANTS**

Any number

**PLAYING TIME**

12-18 minutes

**REQUIRED MATERIALS**

Deck of 12 Freezer Cards

**TO PLAY**

1. Introduce participants to Kurt Lewin's Unfreezing and Refreezing Model of planned change.
2. Go over the learning objective for the game.
3. Explain to players that they are going to be given a deck of Freezer Cards. The deck contains 12 cards (i.e., four Defrosting Cards, four Restructuring Cards, and four Refreezing Cards. Defrosting Cards indicate an original mindset before it was changed, Restructuring Cards constitute a mindset in transition, and Freezing Cards represent a newly formed mindset.
4. Inform participants that the object of the game is to be the first person to correcly place the cards in a matrix containing four rows and three columns. The first column must contain only Defrost Cards, the second only Restructure Cards, and the third only Refreeze Cards. Each row is to contain a Defrost Card, Restructure Card, and a Refreeze Card related to the same topic (e.g., smoking in the workplace).

5. Advise participants that when they think they have all of their cards in the correct rows and columns, they are to call out "Freeze." As soon as someone calls freeze, everyone is to immediately stop playing.
6. Pass out a deck of Freezer Cards to each player.
7. Tell players to begin.
8. As soon as someone calls "Freeze" ask all players to stop playing while you check the person's cards for accuracy.
9. If the freezer cards are correctly placed in the appropriate rows and columns, declare the person the winner of "The Great Siberian Freeze-Off." If the freezer cards are incorrectly placed, continue play until a winner is found.
10. Debrief players. Brainstorm other defrosters and refreezers which could appear on the cards. Have participants make a list of the strategies for unfreezing or refreezing behaviors that they have found to be particularly effective in their organizations. Ask them to discuss which of the two they believe to be the most difficult to accomplish, the unfreezing or refreezing of mindsets. Have players identify mindsets in their organizations which have been the most resistant to change.

**VARIATION**

Play according to the above directions, except use cards containing mindsets the organization would like to change. Replay the game using facilitator-made defrosting and refreezing cards and participant-made restructuring strategy cards. Players must place the defrosting and refreezing cards in the appropriate positions on the matrix, compose a restructuring strategy card for each mindset, and place the strategy cards between the corresponding defrosting and refreezing cards. Each restructuring strategy card should state a means of moving from the old to the new mindset.

**FOR MORE INFORMATION**

Lewin, K. (1951) *Field theory in social science.* New York: Harper.

Answers

| | | |
|---|---|---|
| Most employees should be allowed to smoke at their work stations. | Employees have a right to a healthful work environment. | Employees should not be allowed to smoke at their work stations. |
| Productivity is highest when employees are told how they are to do their jobs and perform their tasks independently of other workers. | Employees are best qualified to make many decisions about their work. Workers can achieve more with and higher quality when working cooperatively. | Employees should have the opportunity to work in self-directed work teams. |
| Computers are expensive toys which cannot be relied on to perform important functions in the workplace. | Because of advances in technology, computers can be relied on to perform many work functions with speed and accuracy. | Few companies can remain competitive without the use of computers. |
| Women are incapable of performing combat duties in the military. | When given the opportunity to do so, it has been shown that women can perform almost any job. | Women should have the opportunity to compete for any job, including those in the military. |

## Freezer Cards

To prepare one deck of Freezer Cards, photocopy the following items on card-stock paper and cut them out.

| | |
|---|---|
| Most employees should be allowed to smoke at their work stations. | Employees have a right to a healthful work environment. |
| Employees should not be allowed to smoke at their work stations. | Productivity is highest when employees are told how they are to do their jobs and perform their tasks independently of other workers. |
| Employees are best qualified to make many decisions about their work. Workers can achieve more and with higher quality when working cooperatively. | Employees should have the opportunity to work in self-directed work teams. |
| Computers are expensive toys which cannot be relied on to perform important functions in the workplace. | Because of advances in technology, computers can be relied on to perform many work functions with speed and accuracy. |

Few companies can remain competitive without the use of computers.

Women are incapable of performing combat duties in the military.

When given the opportunity to do so, it has been shown that women can perform almost any job.

Women should have the opportunity to compete for any job, including those in the military.

# MIND READERS' RALLY

| | |
|---|---|
| **TOPIC** | Gap analysis |

There is often an enormous difference between the mindsets that people speak aloud and that which they actually believe to be true. For example, when a friend asks you what you think of her or his new hairstyle you might say, "Your stylist appears to be very creative." However you may be thinking, "He or She must have created the hairstyles for the Sesame Street muppets."

Such behavior occurs for a variety of reasons. In some cases, people have been brought up to be sensitive to the feelings of others. They don't speak their minds if they think that their comments may offend someone. In other cases people may not say what they think because they fear negative repercussions. For example, they may believe that if they don't go along with the boss they won't get a raise or a promotion. Worse yet, they may lose their job.

At work and at home, things can get quite complicated when individuals take what is said as the person's true opinion. For example, Bill says "That's really a great idea Mary." Mary may go forward spending a great amount of time and energy on an idea that no one really supports. Mary's feelings may be hurt even worse when she finds out that Bill was less than honest with her in the first place.

| | |
|---|---|
| **LEARNING OBJECTIVE** | Players will be able to discern the difference between thoughts that individuals hold in their heads and those they speak aloud. |
| **NUMBER OF PARTICIPANTS** | 12 or more with 6 to10 players on each team |
| **PLAYING TIME** | 12-18 minutes depending upon the number of players |
| **REQUIRED MATERIALS** | Straight pins, felt-tip writing pens, and sets of Mind Reading Cards |
| **TO PLAY** | 1. Introduce players to the concept of spoken versus unspoken mindsets. |

2. Go over the learning objective of the game.
3. Pass out a straight pin and a Mind Reading Card to each player. Circulate felt tip pens around the room.
4. Ask players to carefully read the spoken mindset appearing on their cards.
5. Ask them to pretend that they are the person who spoke the words on their card. Have them imagine something quite different that they might have really been thinking as they spoke these words.
6. Without showing or discussing their inner thoughts with anyone else in the room, direct players to neatly print their true thoughts on the back side of their Mind Reading Card. Ask participants to immediately pin their cards to their blouses or shirts.
7. Divide participants into opposing teams with 6 to 10 players per team. Each team should stand in a straight line approximately eight feet away from any other teams. While remaining in a line formation, half the members of each team should turn around to face the other half. The resulting formation is opposing teams standing in straight parallel lines eight feet apart from one another with half the members of each team facing the remaining half.
8. Explain that the object of the game is to be the first team to correctly guess what teammates have written on the backs of their Mind Reading Cards.
9. Inform participants that when you call "Rally" the player with the smallest shoe size is to begin guessing the unspoken comments the other player has written on the back of her/his card. As soon as one player has correctly guessed what the other has written, then the second player can begin guessing. When the first two facing players have correctly guessed each other's unspoken comments, they go to the rear of their respective lines and the next two players take their turns. Following the order of the first contestants, play alternates between the sides.
10. Inform participants that they are not allowed to give any hints as to what they have written on their cards. They can only answer "Yes" or "No" to guesses of the recorded mindset.
11. Explain that guesses of recorded mindsets do not have to be verbatim quotations of the hidden mindsets. They may be loose translations or paraphrases of what is on the cards.

154

12. As soon as the last player guesses her or his teammates unspoken comment, she or he is to call "Rally." Their team becomes the winning team.

13. Debrief players. Ask players to tell how they knew what to guess regarding the hidden mindsets. Make a list of commonly spoken mindsets around the office. Ask players to furnish hidden mindsets that often accompany these spoken mindsets. Discuss instances in which discrepancies between spoken and unspoken mindsets have interfered with good communication and/or effective decision making. Solicit opinions as to whether discrepancies in spoken and unspoken mindsets are more or less common in certain cultures, industries, or departments. Ask players to account for such differences.

**VARIATION**

Pass out blank Mind Reading Cards to participants. Have them record a mindset which they often think but seldom say. Collect the cards and play the game according to the above directions. However, this time players will record accompanying spoken mindsets on the reverse side of the Mind Reading Cards.

**FOR MORE INFORMATION**

Lewin, K. (1951). *Field theory in social science*. New York: Harper.

# Mind Reading Cards

To prepare one set of Mind Reading Cards, photocopy the following items on card-stock paper and cut them out.

## At Work

| | |
|---|---|
| **1.**<br>To supervisor: It's quite all right. I'll be happy to stay late and work on that report. | **2.**<br>At gathering of coworkers: The 2% raise does keep up with inflation. |
| **3.**<br>To customer: No Mrs. Johnson, I'm not trying to avoid you. I'll be with you as soon as I've finished with this customer who was before you. | **4.**<br>To coworker: You sure get a lot of phone calls at the office. You must have a full social life. |

156

> **5.**
> To coworker: Yes, it is unfortunate that these meetings always seem to be scheduled when you have to be somewhere else.

**At Home**

> **6.**
> To neighbor: Gee, it seems your dog finds the grass greener in my yard.

> **7.**
> To visitor with a child: Little Tommy sure has a strong set of lungs. Maybe he'll be an announcer when he grows up.

> **8.**
> At a friend's home: That certainly is interesting wallpaper in the dining room. I had no idea you were into wild animals.

> **9.**
> To visiting relative: Where did you meet your new beau Aunt Edith? He's much different from the other's you've dated.

10.

At church: Good morning Reverend Morgan. I've never heard Paul's march to Damascus explained in such detail as you did this morning.

# SENGE'S TILES

| | |
|---|---|
| **TOPIC** | Senge's five disciplines |

Learning organizations see themselves as living organisms constantly needing to take new actions in an ever-changing environment. They attempt to take new actions in a more timely manner by speeding up the learning of their individual employees and the organization as a whole. The accelerated learning is achieved by teaching employees critical-thinking skills and helping them learn how to learn and how their organization functions as a system. The concept of the learning organization has come to be closely associated with Peter Senge and his core disciplines for building a learning organization.

**LEARNING OBJECTIVE**

Participants will become familiar with the five disciplines of the learning organization.

**NUMBER OF PARTICIPANTS**

Any number

**PLAYING TIME**

7-9 minutes

**REQUIRED MATERIALS**

Pencils, Learning Organization Tile Sheets, flip chart, and markers

**TO PLAY**

1. Introduce players to Peter Senge's concept of the "learning organization."
2. Go over the learning objective for the game.
3. Explain to players that they are going to play a very brief game that requires them to identify the five disciplines of the learning organization.
4. Pass out pencils and copies of the Learning Organization Tile Sheet to each participant.
5. Ask players not to pick up their pencils and begin writing until you call "Begin."
6. Read aloud the directions appearing at the top of the tile sheet.
7. Call "Begin."
8. Five minutes later call "Stop."
9. Read aloud the answers to the puzzle while players correct their own tile sheets.

10. Have the participants who filled in all five answers correctly stand. Declare them winners.
11. Debrief players. Go over the meanings of the five disciplines (see Chapter One). Ask participants to identify which of the five disciplines they believe to be the most important to today's organizations. Have players discuss which of the disciplines their organizations should set as a high priority. On a flip chart, list potential strategies for implementing these learning disciplines.

**VARIATION**     Instead of playing the game as individual contestants, play the game as teams attempting to be the first to solve the puzzle. To make the game more challenging, have players fill in the blank spaces without the benefit of the tiles. If an organization has come up with its own set of learning principles for becoming a learning organization, they might be substituted for Senge's five disciplines and the game played according to the above directions.

**FOR MORE INFORMATION**     Senge, P. M. (1990). *The fifth discipline.* New York: Doubleday/Currency

Answer

1. Systems Thinking
2. Personal Mastery
3. Mental Models
4. Building Shared Vision
5. Team Learning

## Learning Organization Tile Sheet

**Directions:** Using the letter blocks on the left, fill in the missing letters in the five disciplines of the learning organization on the right.

| | |
|---|---|
| AL | IN |
| AL | LS |
| AM | MA |
| AR | MS |
| EN | NG |
| ER | OD |
| HA | RS |
| HI | SI |
| IL | YS |
| IN | |

**1.** S ☐ TE ☐

T ☐ NK ☐ G

**2.** PE ☐ ON ☐

☐ ST ☐ Y

**3.** M ☐ T ☐

M ☐ E ☐

**4.** BU ☐ DI ☐ S ☐ RED

VI ☐ ON

**5.** TE ☐

LE ☐ N ☐ G

# SHIFTER

| | |
|---|---|
| **TOPIC** | Paradigm shifts |

Paradigms are mental frames of reference. They can include such concepts as job, client, employee involvement, customer service, or product quality. Because paradigms set and attach mental boundaries to these concepts, they have a major effect on the ways organizations operate. For example, who an organization considers and doesn't consider as clients greatly impacts on how it goes about its business.

When the meaning of a concept is changed, it is commonly referred to as a paradigm shift. For example, the concept of a computer started out as being a machine for rapidly making complex calculations. It is now considered a multipurpose communications tool.

**LEARNING OBJECTIVE**

Participants will be able to identify paradigm shifts occurring in their organizations.

**NUMBER OF PARTICIPANTS**

Eight or more divided into groups of four players

**PLAYING TIME**

8-10 minutes

**REQUIRED MATERIALS**

Paradigm Shifter Court Squares and a roll of double-sided tape

**TO PLAY**

1. Introduce players to the concept of a "paradigm."
2. Go over the learning objective for the game.
3. Tell players that they are about to begin a game similar to the popular game of "Twister." Each team will make their way to one of the Shifter Courts set up about the room. Each court contains four paradigm shifts. One of the squares on the court contains the old paradigm and another square contains the new paradigm.
4. Explain that members of each team must physically connect the old with the new paradigm by placing their left foot on the old and their right on the new paradigm. The team which correctly connects all four paradigms first will become winners.
5. Divide participants into groups of four.

6. Direct groups to go to an unoccupied Shifter Court.
7. Call "Begin."
8. As soon as one group finishes, check the accuracy of their connections.
9. Declare the group who is the first to correctly make all four connections "winners."
10. Debrief players. Ask participants to identify evidence of the paradigm shifts appearing on the Shifter Court. Discuss paradigm shifts which have occurred in players' companies during the past five years. Ask players to elaborate on some of the organization or employee behavior changes that ensued from the paradigm shifts. List paradigms existing in the workplace that need redefining. Discuss what these paradigms might look like if they were shifted to something more in keeping with today's business practices.

**VARIATION**    Rather than setting up paradigm Shifter Courts around the room, make a three-by-three Paradigm Shifter Grid (similar to the chart below). Use the paradigm shift examples listed in the game or make up your own. Pass out copies of the grids to players. Using their fingers, see who can correctly connect the most shifts. Take care to place the paradigm pairs on the grid so that they can actually be connected using eight fingers. Declare those who can correctly connect the shifts within a two-minute period, winners.

**FOR MORE**
**INFORMATION**    Barker, J. A. (1992). *Paradigms: The business of discovering the future*. New York: HarperCollins Publishers, Inc.

Answers:    Marriage-Cohabitation, Employee-Entrepreneur, Hierarchical-Matrix, Postal Service-Internet

## Paradigm Shifter Court

To construct one Paradigm Shifter Court, photocopy the large titles on card-stock paper. Tape the tiles to the floor one foot apart in the following the pattern.

| Marriage | Postal Service | Cohabitation |
|----------|----------------|--------------|
| Employee | Free Space | Internet |
| Hierarchical | Entrepreneur | Matrix |

# Free Space

# Marriage

# Postal Service

# Cohabitation

# Employee

# Internet

# Hierarchical

# Entrepreneur

# Matrix

# WALKING THE TALK

**TOPIC**

Becoming a learning organization

There are several steps a company can take to become a more effective learning organization. They include: (1) Analyzing the current culture to determine how new learning occurs and is rewarded in the company; (2)beginning to reward employees for thinking (not just agreeing with the boss or colleagues); (3)learning how to become better at learning; (4)mastering the five learning disciplines (see Chapter One); (5)creating a vision of what the new learning organization will look like; (6)making a plan to move the company from where it is now in terms of its learning to where it would like to be in the future; and (7)integrating the vision and strategies for achieving the vision into all the organization systems.

**LEARNING OBJECTIVE**

Participants will be able to take some of the steps necessary to make their company a learning organization.

**NUMBER OF PARTICIPANTS**

14 or more in multiples of 7

**PLAYING TIME**

15-20 minutes

**REQUIRED MATERIALS**

Sets of Footprints and masking tape

**TO PLAY**

1. Explain to participants some of the key steps an organization might take on its way to becoming a learning organization.
2. Go over the learning objective for the game.
3. Explain to participants that they are about to play a game (Walk the Talk) which will challenge their abilities to walk the above seven steps to becoming a learning organization.
4. Divide participants into groups of seven players each.
5. Have groups take their places around the room. Each group should be at least 10 feet away from any other group.
6. Supply each group with a set of footprints and a roll of masking tape.

7. Direct each group to tape the footprints to the floor in the correct order, approximately one foot apart from each other.

8. Have players remove their shoes and line up in a straight line behind the first footprint (Analyze the Culture).

9. Explain that the game is played with the first player stepping on the first footprint, stopping long enough to shout the step (i.e., Analyze the Culture), and continuing walking on the remaining footprints (i.e., footprints two through seven). The second player begins stepping her or his way through the footprints as soon as the previous player has stepped off footprint seven. She or he stops on footprint two and shouts out that step (i.e., Reward Thinking) and then continues on through the remaining steps. The next player repeats the process stopping on footprint three.

10. Make sure that everyone understands that players must step on every footprint but they are to stop and call out only their footprint number. Their number is determined by their position in the line. The first person in the line is number one and the last person is number seven.

11. Inform players that if any player calls out the wrong footprint, neglects to step on all seven footprints, or begins stepping on footprint one before the previous player has removed her or his foot from the last footprint, the team must start all over again beginning with the first player.

12. Advise players that the team that first completes its walk is to call out "Walk the Talk." That team will be the winners.

13. Tell players to begin.

14. Declare the team who completes their walk first, winners.

15. Debrief players. Ask participants to discuss some of the steps their organization has taken to become a more effective learning organization. Divide players into small groups according to the seven steps. Have them brainstorm and bring back to the larger group ideas for accomplishing their particular step.

**VARIATION**  (1) Have groups come up with their own steps and play the game according to the above directions. (2) Play the game according to the above directions except have players stop and call out the name of each step. (3) Place footprints facedown all around the room. Give players three minutes to collect all seven footprints. Declare these players winners.

**FOR MORE INFORMATION**   Kline, P. & Saunders, B. (1993). *Ten steps to a learning organization.* Arlington, VA: Great Ocean Publishers, Inc.

Answers
Step 1   Analyze the culture
Step 2   Reward thinking
Step 3   Learn how to learn
Step 4   Master the five disciplines
Step 5   Create a vision
Step 6   Make a travel plan
Step 7   Start your systems

### Foot Prints

To make one set of Foot Prints, photocopy the following items on card-stock paper and cut them out.

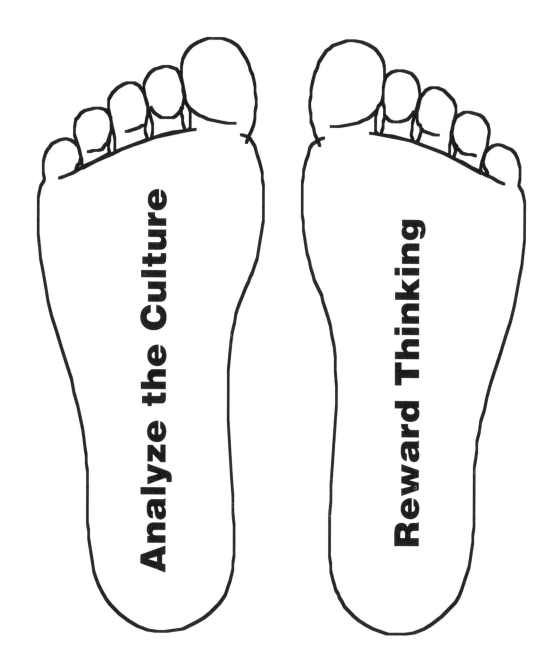

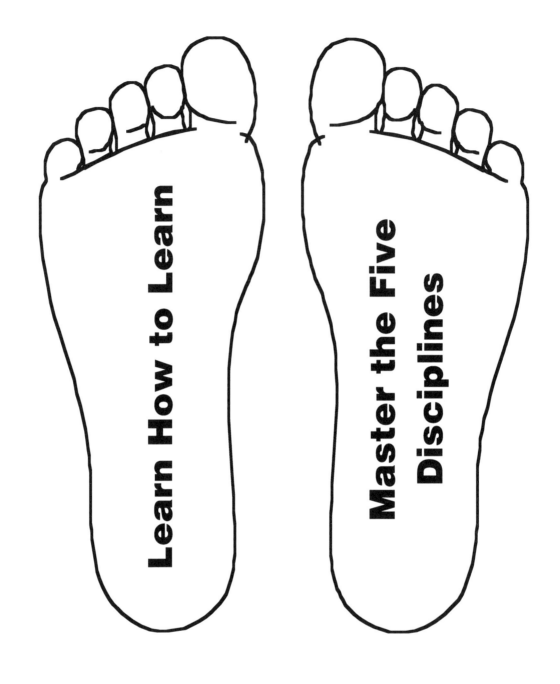

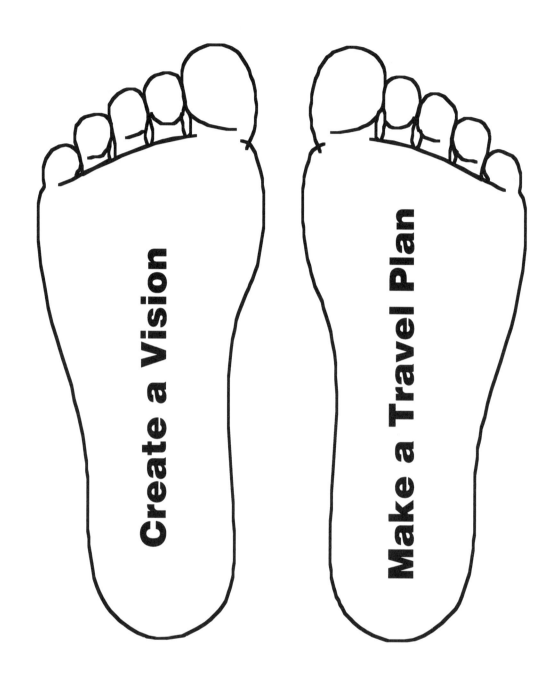

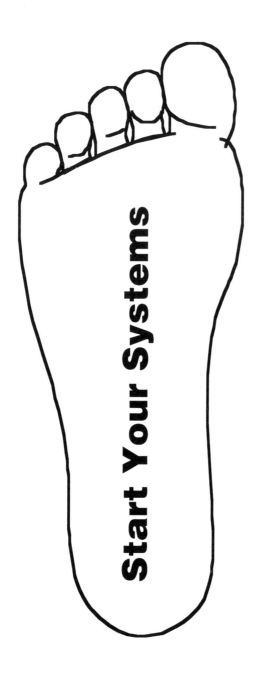

Start Your Systems

# WHO IN OD AM I

**TOPIC**            Organization development experts and their models

Several management pioneers have made notable contributions to the field of organization development. Current writers on the subject of the learning organization have borrowed and built upon the ideas of these pioneers. An appreciation of the work of these management pioneers is essential to fashioning a learning organization (see the Briefing Sheet in this game).

**LEARNING OBJECTIVE**            Participants will become familiar with the contributions of the pioneers in organization development.

**NUMBER OF PARTICIPANTS**            Groups of three to five players

**PLAYING TIME**            15-30 minutes, depending upon the number of players

**REQUIRED MATERIALS**            OD Clue Cards, Briefing Sheets, flip chart, and markers

**TO PLAY**
1. Introduce players to the concept of organization development.
2. Pass out Briefing Sheets to participants. Briefly discuss contributions of each individual to the field of organization development.
3. Go over the learning objective for the game.
4. Explain to participants that they are about to play a game similar to 20 Questions. However, in this case there will only be five questions.
5. Divide participants into small groups of three to five players.
6. Instruct players to stand, place their Briefing Sheets on their chairs, and sit on them. They are not to look at these sheets until the game is over.
7. Provide each group with a deck of OD Clue Cards. Ask one member of each group to shuffle the cards and place them facedown in the center of the group.
8. Direct the person to the left of the shuffler to pick up the top card from the pile and identify herself or himself by saying, "I am an OD expert. Who am I?"
9. Explain that the person on the expert's left is to choose a number between one and five. The expert

will then read the clue that corresponds to that number.

10. Tell the players that the person on the expert's left then has a chance to guess the name of the famous person being described. If the guess is correct, the person receives the card. If incorrect, the expert reads the next clue to the next player. She or he then has a chance to guess.

11. Continue reading the clues in order to each player moving in a clockwise direction until someone guesses correctly, thus receiving the card. After the reader reaches clue five, she or he should start with clue one. If no one correctly identifies the expert after all clues have been read, the expert reading the card identifies herself or himself and gets to keep the card.

12. Explain that the person on the expert's left will then pick a card from the pile (becoming the new expert) and begin the process again.

13. Advise players that the winners will be the first person in each group who collects two OD Clue Cards.

14. After a winner has emerged in each group, have that person stand to be recognized.

15. Debrief players. Have participants list the OD experts on the briefing sheets who they were familiar with prior to the game. Discuss why they may have been familiar with these experts and not with others. On a flip chart, list OD concepts from the Briefing Sheet that have been applied in their organization. Ask each participant to identify a concept on the Briefing Sheet which has not been applied in their organization, but which they believe would benefit their company.

**VARIATION**

Make up briefing sheets with the names and contributions of individuals in your organization who have come up with and/or implemented concepts which have caused your organization to develop over time. Play the game according to the above directions using your newly created Briefing Sheet. Change the name of the game to Who in (your company name) Am I?

**FOR MORE INFORMATION**

Smith, C.L. (1992, February). The human side of business.
*Training*, 29 (2), 37-40.
Dumaine, B. (1994, October). Mr. learning organization. *Fortune*, 130 (8), 147-157.
Straub, D. (Ed.). *Contemporary authors, new revision series*. Detroit, MI: Gale Research Inc.
Locker, F. (Ed.). *Contemporary authors*. Detroit, MI: Gale Research Inc.

# Briefing Sheet

## Chris Argyris

Chris Argyris is known for his application of behavioral sciences to organization life and the double loop learning concept. He believes that organizations can improve their performance by engaging in double loop learning, a process whereby a company looks at the reasons for its past successes and failures. He also encourages CEOs to learn from their past mistakes by writing case studies of themselves. Argyris sees three critical roles for OD consultants: aiding clients in collecting data about the organization, helping clients in making free/informed choices about data collected, and assisting clients in becoming committed to their choices. Furthermore, he believes that effective OD consultants develop generalization in four key areas -- primary tasks of an interventionist, qualities needed by the interventionists, conditions faced by interventionist, and possible awkward adaptations the interventionists might face. Some of Argyris's best known books include, *On Organizational Learning, Increasing Leadership Effectiveness, Intervention, Theory and Method*, and *Integrating the Individual and the Organization.*

## Robert Blake

Robert Blake is known for formulating the Managerial Grid, Scientific Methods, Inc., and the Synergogic Learning Theory. His ever popular Managerial Grid is used to plot a manager's behavior on a grid with respect to her or his attention to people and tasks. His synergogic learning theory attempts to combine good pedagogical instructional practices with good andragogical practices. Blake was among the first to apply the scientific method to studying and resolving intergroup conflicts in business and industry. Together with his well-known partner Jane Mouton, he co-authored many books including *Group Dynamics, Key to Decision Making, Synergogy*, and *The Managerial Grid.*

# Briefing Sheet
(continued)

## Kenneth H. Blanchard

Kenneth H. Blanchard and Paul Hersey are responsible for deriving the leadership model now titled situational leadership. The model shows the need for changes in leadership based on the current needs of an organization. His Participative Change model illustrates how the use of "personal power" causes change in knowledge, followed by change in attitudes, then individual behavior change, and finally change in group behavior. His Coerced Change model demonstrates how the use of "position power" causes change in group behavior, followed by individual behavior change, then attitudinal change, and finally change in knowledge. Blanchard's Time and Difficulty model shows that making knowledge changes is not difficult nor time consuming compared to changing group behavior. While authoring and co-authoring such works as *Management of Organizational Behavior* and *Organizational Change Through Effective Leadership*, he is probably best know for his management classic *The One Minute Manager* and Blanchard Training and Development Company.

## W. Warner Burke

W. Warner Burke considers organization development a continuous process of learning and change. He is among the first authors to use the term organization development in his writings. As the chief architect of NASA's Senior Executive Program he wrote behavioral descriptions of 24 different management practices. In his discussions on the relationship of management development to organization development he compares and contrasts the two interventions on six different dimensions -- goals, reasons for initiating change, difficulties in initiating change, strategies for producing change, time frame and staff requirements, and problems and criticisms. In 1993 he was recognized for his many years of OD practice when he received the Organizational Development Professional Practice Area Award for Excellence from the American Society for Training and Development. Burke is perhaps best known for his books describing the practice of organization development; *The Cutting Edge: Current Theory and Practice in Organizational Development* and *Organizational Development: A Process of Learning and Changing*.

# Briefing Sheet
### (continued)

### Kurt Lewin

Kurt Lewin was a social psychologist considered to be one of the early founders in the field of organization development. He is credited with coining the term "change agent" which characterizes the central role of the OD consultant. He also originated the process of "action research" which is similar to applied research and at the core of all OD practice. Action research is interventionist and produces ideas for change. Lewin was a great proponent of experiential learning which actively engages participants in practical exercises as opposed to passive listening. He was convinced that before new behavior could be acquired, old behaviors must be "unfrozen." His most noted work may be his force-field analysis model which provides change agents a way of examining forces working for and against change. He referred to these forces as "driving" and "restraining" forces.

### Edgar Henry Schein

Schein is one of the foremost experts on organization change. He believes that in order to change an organization you must first gain an understanding of its culture. In his book, *Organizational Culture and Leadership,* he details ways to gain an understanding of a company's culture. He is well known for his six-stage problem solving model used in organization development consulting. The steps are: problem formulation, producing proposals for solution, forecasting consequences (testing proposals), action planning, taking action steps, and evaluating outcomes. He has also developed an extensive career development model which takes into account the development stage of both the employee and that of the employing organization. Schein holds that "career anchors both drive and constrain career choices and decisions." He recognizes such common career anchors as technical/functional competence (concern with exercising technical abilities), managerial competence (concern with task, challenge, and responsibility), security and stability (concern with establishing trust in the organization), creativity (concern with creating a product or process), and autonomy (concern with freedom from organizational constraints). He sees many benefits in fusing the attitudes and assumptions of organization development and clinical therapy.

# Briefing Sheet
### (continued)

### Peter Senge

Peter Senge would have all companies become "learning organizations." He believes that organizations become learning organizations by practicing five disciplines. These disciplines are systems thinking, personal mastery, mental models, shared vision, and team learning. His own personal vision is not just to change corporate America but to change the world. In his organization learning consulting practice he makes frequent use of a learning organization approach known as "dialogue." The process involves a variety of exercises (e.g., Container) that are designed to open up communication. Senge believes that prior to becoming a part of a learning organization, employees must first experience change in their own personal lives.

# OD Clue Cards

To prepare one deck of OD Clue Cards, photocopy the following items on card-stock paper and cut them out.

## Chris Argyris

1. I am famous for my work titled *On Organizational Learning* published in 1992.
2. I coined the term "double loop learning."
3. I identify three major roles for OD consultants.
4. I describe four areas were OD consultants need to make generalizations before intervening.
5. I encourage CEO s to learn about their mistakes by writing case studies about themselves.

## Robert R. Blake

1. I was inducted into the Human Resource Development Hall of Fame on December 9, 1987.
2. I strongly advocate the use of the scientific method in the understanding and resolution of intergroup conflicts.
3. I believe that learning can be made more effective through the combined use of good pedagogical and andragogical concepts.
4. I co-authored numerous publications with Jane Mouton.
5. My partner and I created the Managerial Grid.

## Kenneth Blanchard

1. I have demonstrated in my Time and Difficulty model that changing an employee's knowledge is neither difficult nor very time consuming compared to changing group behavior.
2. My Participative Change model illustrates how personal power can be used to affect changes in an organization.
3. My Coerced Change model illustrates how position power can be used to affect changes in an organization.
4. Paul Hersey and I are responsible for a leadership model initially called the Life Cycle Theory of Leadership Behavior, later referred to as Situational Leadership.
5. I am known as the "one-minute manager."

## W. Warner Burke

1. I believe organization development to be a continuous process of learning and changing.
2. I am among the very first authors to use the term organization development in my writings.
3. I have identified and described 24 specific management practices.
4. I have contrasted and compared management development with organization development.
5. I am perhaps best know for my books describing the practice of organization development; *The Cutting Edge: Current Theory and Practice in Organizational Development* and *Organizational Development: A process of Learning and Changing.*

| **Kurt Lewin** |
| --- |

1. I am considered one of the founding fathers of organization development practice.
2. I coined the term "change agent."
3. I originated the concept of "action research."
4. I am known for my learning model which involves the unfreezing of old and refreezing of new behaviors.
5. I am, perhaps, best known for my technique commonly referred to as "force field analysis."

| **Edgar H. Schein** |
| --- |

1. I have conceived a six step problem solving model which is often used in organization development consulting.
2. I believe that a leader must understand an organization's culture in order to change it.
3. I coined the term "career anchors."
4. I have created a career development model which takes into account the development needs of an employee as well as the needs of the employing organization.
5. I advocate fusing the attitudes of clinical therapy and organization development.

## Peter Senge

1. I am a strong advocate of the learning organization.
2. I believe that to become a part of a learning organization employees must first experience change in their own personal lives.
3. I hold that companies become learning organizations by practicing five disciplines.
4. I advocate a learning organization approach known as "dialogue."
5. My own personal vision is not only to change corporate America into learning organizations but to actually change the world.

# Chapter Five

# Group Portraits Games

# BENCH PINCHING

| | |
|---|---|
| **TOPIC** | Benchmarking |

Benchmarking involves assessing one's own organization's practices and then comparing them to those of another company. The process is usually part of a quality improvement effort that focuses on a particular area of a company's business. For example, a company may choose to match a competitor's 98% customer satisfaction rate or its 1 1/2% product return rate. The company to which practices are compared is often a competitor or one that is recognized as a leader in its field.

**LEARNING OBJECTIVE**

Participants will be able to identify company processes that are appropriate for benchmarking.

**NUMBER OF PARTICIPANTS**

Any number divided into groups of four or five players

**PLAYING TIME**  12-17 minutes

**REQUIRED MATERIALS**

Benchmarking Activity Cards, flip chart, and markers

**TO PLAY**

1. Explain to participants the practice of benchmarking.
2. Go over the learning objective for the game.
3. Advise participants that they are going to be divided into groups of four to five players. Once in their groups they will be handed a Benchmarking Activity Card. Each person in the group will perform the activity on the card. Afterward members will decide who in their group is best at performing the designated activity.
4. Divide participants into small groups of four to five players.
5. Give one person in each group a Benchmarking Activity Card. Ask these individuals to read the contents of the card aloud to group members.
6. Request that the readers of the activity perform the specified activity for their respective groups.
7. Continuing around the groups in a clockwise direction, have remaining members of groups perform the same activity.

8. Once everyone in a group has performed the benchmarking activity, ask them to softly pinch the person on the right arm who they believe did the best job of performing the activity.
9. Declare the person receiving the most pinches in each group the winners.
10. Ask the winners to provide the members in their group with a one-minute training session on the best way to perform their group's benchmarking activity.
11. Debrief players. On a flip chart, list practices in their organizations that players feel lend themselves to benchmarking. Select a practice which holds critical importance to the success of most companies. Identify individuals, teams, departments, or companies which perform this practice exceptionally well. Specify performance standards that could be used for comparative purposes.

**VARIATION**

Construct your own Benchmarking Activity Cards using three to five activities that players actually perform on the job. Have three volunteers from the audience come forward to perform one of the activities. Ask members of the audience to come forward and softly pinch the best performer on the right arm. Declare the performer receiving the most pinches the winner and company benchmarker. Call a new set of contestants forward and repeat the process three or four more times.

**FOR MORE INFORMATION**

Spendolini, M. (1992) *The benchmarking book.* New York: AMACOM.

**Benchmarking Activity Cards**

To make a set of Benchmarking Activity Cards, photocopy the following items on card-stock paper and cut them out.

| **Body Musicians** |
| --- |
| Use a part or parts of your body as a musical instrument to play the chorus of O' Suzannah. If you wish, you or other members in your group may sing along. |

| **Comedians** |
| --- |
| Think of the funniest joke you have ever heard in your entire life. Tell the joke to members of your group. No obscene, sexist, or racist jokes please. |

| **Flirters** |
| --- |
| Pretend that you are standing in a small group at a cocktail party drinking a glass of wine. You are attracted to a person standing near you. Please flirt with this person in a manner that will most surely gain her or his attention. |

## Impersonators

Think of a popular television or film screen personality. Give a brief impersonation of the celebrity. Wait until after your impersonation to tell the name of the individual.

## Prevaricators

Pretend you are among the finalists at the National Prevaricator Association's Annual Liars Contest. $10,000 in prize money is riding on your ability to tell the most outrageous lie of your life. Tell the biggest lie you can possibly imagine.

# DIMESWORTH BUY IN

| TOPIC | Vision selling |
|---|---|

The imagined future an organization sees for itself is more apt to be realized if most employees are willing to take ownership of the vision. Getting employees to buy into a vision often requires more than just getting input from workers. It typically requires some selling on the part of managers and other employees.

**LEARNING OBJECTIVE**

Participants will be able to generate strategies for selling a company's vision.

**NUMBER OF PARTICIPANTS**

Any number

**PLAYING TIME**

15-20 minutes

**REQUIRED MATERIALS**

Dimesworth Buy In case study, vision money, three sets of felt-tip markers of various colors, three large pieces of poster board, and a roll of masking tape.

**TO PLAY**

1. Introduce players to the concept of selling a company's vision.
2. Go over the learning objective for the game.
3. Explain to players that most of them will soon be presented with three visions into which they can invest money. They can invest all of their money in one vision or split their investment up among the various visions.
4. Advise participants that three players will take on the role of vision leaders. As vision leaders, they will create a new vision for the Dimesworth Discount Department Store chain, draw a visual representation of the vision on a piece of poster board, and attempt to sell the vision to other players.
5. Tell players that the vision leader who receives the most vision money during the game becomes the winning leader.
6. Select three vision leaders from the audience. Provide each a copy of the case study Dimesworth Buy In, a set of color felt-tip markers, and a large piece of poster board.

7. Inform vision leaders they have five minutes to create their visions. Have them go to various corners of the room or out in the hall to create their masterpieces.

8. While the vision tellers are creating their visions, read the Dimesworth Buy In case study to the remaining players.

9. Pass out $500 in vision money to each participant.

10. Explain that if they invested in the winning vision they will receive back twice the amount they invested. No returns will be realized on the remaining two visions. The investors with the most vision money at the end of the game will be considered winners.

11. Have vision leaders tape up their visions on three separate walls in the room. Give the leaders 30 seconds each to explain their vision.

12. Give participants six minutes to walk around the room and invest in the various visions. Vision leaders will continue selling their visions as well as collecting investment money from investors. Investors must keep track of how much they invested in each vision.

13. Have investors vote on the best vision.

14. Declare the vision leader who created that vision the winning vision leader.

15. Ask investors to double the amount of money they invested in the winning vision and add it to the amount of vision money still in their possession.

16. Declare the persons with the most vision money, winners.

17. Debrief players. Ask participants which vision they voted for and why they thought it was the best vision. On a flip chart, list two good selling points presented by each vision leader. Discuss other selling points vision leaders might have found effective in selling their particular vision. Have participants elaborate on some of the strategies their company has effectively used in selling or promoting its vision.

**VARIATION**

Collect vision statements from various units within an organization. Select a corresponding number of vision leaders to create a picture of the vision on a poster board. Play the remaining portion of the game according to the above directions.

**FOR MORE INFORMATION**     Goman, C. (1991). *Managing for commitment.* Menlo Park, CA: Crisp Publications, Inc.
Heim, P. & Chapman, E. (1990). *Learning to lead.* Menlo Park, CA: Crisp Publications, Inc.

## Dimesworth Buy In

Dimesworth Discount Department Stores is a small company with three stores in and around the metropolitan Chicago area. Dimesworth started out as one small store in an old established downtown section of the city. In the 20 years of its existence, Dimesworth stores have grown to large, modern, freestanding, and highly successful businesses which anchor shopping plazas. Recently, a monolithic national discount chain has announced plans to move into the area with a megastore. In order to remain in business and compete with the much larger chain store, what would be the best vision for Dimesworth to implement?

## Vision Money

To make a sufficient stash of vision money, photocopy ample amounts of the following items. There should be enough money to provide each player with $500 and each vision leader with an ample supply for making change.

| | | |
|---|---|---|
| **20** | | **20** |
| Vision | 👁 | Money |
| **20** | | **20** |

| | | |
|---|---|---|
| **50** | | **50** |
| Vision | 👁 | Money |
| **50** | | **50** |

| | | |
|---|---|---|
| **100** | | **100** |
| Vision | 👁 | Money |
| **100** | | **100** |

# FIVE-STAR GOALS

**TOPIC**      Effective goals

Goals serve as "milemarkers" along the route to achieving organization and/or personal visions. In establishing these intermediate visions of where we would like to be at a given time, it is important to keep certain goal criteria in mind. Goals should be **s**pecific (the results can be observed), **m**easurable (results can be quantified), **a**ttainable (it is possible to reach the goal), **r**elevant (goal pertains to a larger mission or vision), and **t**rackable (possible to chart progress toward the goal over time).

**LEARNING OBJECTIVE**      Participants will be able to set SMART goals.

**NUMBER OF PARTICIPANTS**      Any number

**PLAYING TIME**      6-10 minutes

**REQUIRED MATERIALS**      Pencils and Five-Star Goals worksheets

**TO PLAY**
1. Introduce players to the five criteria for SMART goals.
2. Go over the learning objective for the game.
3. Pass out a pencil and a copy of the Five-Star Goals worksheet to each player.
4. Go over the directions at the top of the worksheet.
5. Explain to players that they are not to pick up their pencils and begin filling in the worksheet until you say "Go."
6. Tell players they only have two minutes to complete the worksheet.
7. Call "Go."
8. Two minutes later call "Stop."
9. Have players correct their worksheets as you give them the right answers.
10. Declare players who matched all five goals correctly the winners and "very smart goal setters."
11. Debrief players. Have the group rank order the SMART goal criteria from one to five in terms of their importance to setting organization goals. Rank one the most important and five the least

important. Discuss which of the criteria are most difficult to address when setting goals. Have players share some of their own criteria for setting goals.

**VARIATION**

Play the game with personal goals written by participants. Replace the SMART goal criteria with CLASS goal criteria. The letters in CLASS stand for **c**ompatible (achieving the goal would contribute to, not conflict with, the goals of the company), **l**iving (the goal is something to which you are strongly committed and energized by), **a**ttainable (you can actually achieve the goal), **s**pecific (the goal is clearly stated and easily understood by others), and **s**atisfying (the completion of the goal will bring you immense inner satisfaction).

**FOR MORE INFORMATION**

Conlow, R. (1991). *Excellence in management.* Menlo Park, CA: Crisp Publications, Inc.

Answers: Specific-C, Measureable-B, Attainable-D, Relevant-A, Trackable-E.

**Five Star Goals**

**Directions:** A small bank in a community of 10,000 residents wishes to increase its business through improved customer service. Carefully read each of the bank's five customer service goals listed below. Record the letter of each goal under the SMART goal criteria it most closely matches. Keep in mind that there is only one correct solution to the puzzle.

A   To bring in almost all of the banking customers available.
B   To increase our customer satisfaction rating by 5 percent.
C   To provide one-day loan service to our large-account customers.
D   To provide our customers with improved service.
E   To reduce the number of monthly customer complaints by 12 percent over a six-month period.

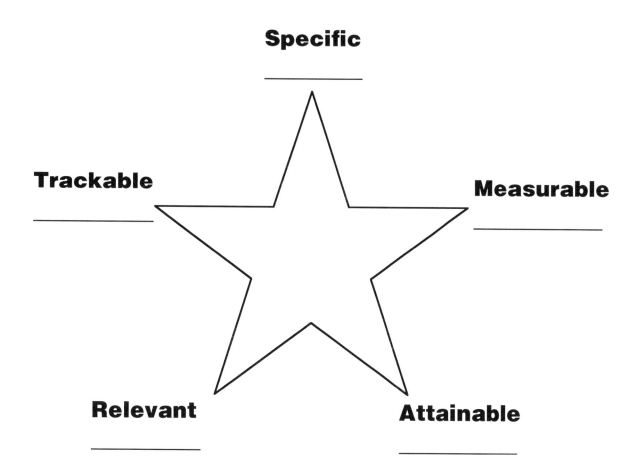

# HANDS UP

**TOPIC**     Personal visions

Personal visions are what individual workers would like their lives to be like in the future. It includes aspects of their personal lives as well as desired employment opportunities. Taking the form of hidden agendas, personal visions can greatly impact decisions made by team members. When personal visions run contrary to the organization's vision, individual commitment to the organization vision may lapse.

**LEARNING OBJECTIVE**     Participants will be able to articulate their personal visions to others.

**NUMBER OF PARTICIPANTS**     Any even number of participants

**PLAYING TIME**     15-20 minutes

**REQUIRED MATERIALS**     Paper, pencils, and Palm Reader's Guide

**TO PLAY**
1. Introduce players to the concept of personal vision.
2. Go over the learning objective for the game.
3. Explain to players that they are going to play a game that involves writing a brief personal vision and then having another player acting as a palm reader attempt to "read" that vision.
4. Advise players that they will both write a personal vision and attempt to foretell the personal vision of a partner.
5. Inform participants that points will be awarded for predicting events that are in a partner's vision.
6. Provide players with pencils and paper on which to write their personal career visions. Ask them to write down what they would prefer to be doing 5 to 10 years from now. They can include such things as where they will be working, what city or area of the country they will be working in, any future changes in career, promotions, significant accomplishments, and setbacks.
7. Allow five minutes for the writing of personal visions.

8. Pass out copies of the Palm Reader's Guide to all participants.
9. Give players two minutes to read over the directions. Answer any questions that arise.
10. Have participants pair up, preferably with someone they know.
11. Have players foretell each other's visions by reading the palms of one another's hands.
12. Ask pairs to collectively add up the number of predictions made in their palm readings that also appeared in their personal vision statements.
13. Declare the partners with the most matches the winning palm readers.
14. Debrief players. Discuss the value of having a personal vision. Elaborate on the merits of writing a personal vision before and after your company prepares its vision statement. List some measures a team can take to reduce the chances of hidden career visions having undue influence on its decisions. Ask individuals to gauge how closely their personal visions align with those of their department or company.

**VARIATION**

Instead of writing personal vision statements prior to the palm reading, do the palm reading first. Divide participants into pairs and have one person read the other's palm. Ask the readers to be very creative and imaginative. Encourage them to come up with futures their partner might not otherwise imagine. Ask the player whose palm has just been read to write down ideas mentioned in the reading that they would like to include in a personal vision statement. Declare palm readers with the most recorded ideas winners of round one. For round two, have palm readers switch partners and reverse roles (they will now be clients having their palms read). Repeat the same steps used in round one.

**FOR MORE INFORMATION**

Senge, P. M. (1990). *The fifth discipline.* New York: Doubleday/Currency

## Palm Readers Guide

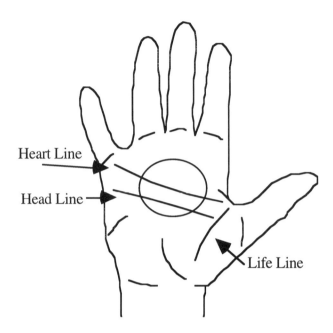

Heart Line

Head Line

Life Line

TO INTERPRET THE PALMS-- When reading the palms remember that you should weave a story around your interpretation of all the lines and palm area. Be creative and let your imagination run wild. Preface each observation with the words "I see..." The drawing of the hand will give you an idea of where the lines are located on the palm. The following is a general, but totally made up, description of what each line and area indicates.

1. HEAD LINE -- The longer and straighter this line is, the higher the position in a company or chosen career the person will achieve. Broken or wavy lines may indicate struggles to get ahead. You may also read other markings on the line in your own creative style (lines intersecting the main line, x's on it, circles in it, etc.).

2. HEART LINE -- Here the emphasis will again be on the length and straightness of the line. A relatively short line could mean the person is more interested in learning a variety of things, but not mastering any one area. A long line might mean the person is focused on one area of expertise. Breaks in the line might mean a short attention span, jumping from one thing to another. Be creative in interpreting markings on this line as well.

3. LIFELINE -- This line relates to longevity with a company or in a career. You decide what is the case for the person whose palm you're reading. Markings along this line are open to your creative genius for interpretation.

4.  DEPTH OF PALM -- Here we have the capacity to hold money (i.e., monetary rewards). As a rule, the deeper the palm, the more money it will hold. This may be read in conjunction with the other hand lines. For example, perhaps a person has a deep palm and a broken wavy heart line. You might state that the person will make lots of money but waste it. The possibilities are limited only by your imagination.

# MYSTERY MISSIONS

| | |
|---|---|
| **TOPIC** | Mission statements |

A mission statement proclaims a company's purpose or reason for existing. Coming up with a clear mission statement is often the very first step in creating a strategic plan. A good mission statement reveals the kind of business the organization expects to be in the foreseeable future. It may also include the company's key objectives and how it hopes to achieve them. The mission statement should be succinct so that it can be easily communicated throughout the organization.

**LEARNING OBJECTIVE**

Participants will be able to construct an appropriate mission statement for their team, department, or company.

**NUMBER OF PARTICIPANTS**

Any number

**PLAYING TIME**

10-12 minutes

**REQUIRED MATERIALS**

Pencils and Mystery Mission Board, flip chart, and markers

**TO PLAY**

1. Discuss the concept of the mission statement.
2. Go over the learning objective for the game.
3. Explain to players that they are now going to test their knowledge of mission statements with a game similar to tic-tac-toe.
4. Pass out pencils and copies of the Mystery Mission Board.
5. Explain that the object of the game is to get three correct answers in a row (e.g., three in a row horizontally, vertically, or diagonally) and/or to get four correct answers, one in each corner of the board.
6. Give players two minutes to fill in their answers.
7. Give the correct answers, having participants check their own responses.
8. Declare players with the most tic-tac-toes winners.
9. Debrief players. Discuss which company missions most surprised players. Use selected missions to speculate on what the mission reveals about the

company's culture. On a flip chart, list criteria for a good mission. Identify which companies in the game best meet the criteria. Ask participants to recite and evaluate their company's mission according to the group's criteria.

**VARIATION**  Instead of having players fill in all squares, have them fill in only three squares in a row or the four corner squares. Another variation would be to use mission statements from various departments in your organization to play the game according to the above rules.

**FOR MORE INFORMATION**  Calfee, D. L. (January, 1993). Get your mission statement working! *Management Review,* 82, (1), p. 54. Krohe, J. Jr. (July/August, 1995). Do you really need a mission statement? *Across the Board,* 32, (7), p. 6.

Answers: Row 1, A, D, L , Row 2 Q, K, I , Row 3 B, F, P

# Mystery Mission Board

**Directions**: First read each of the nine mission statements in the boxes below. On the line in each box write the letter of the company (A-R) to which you believe the mission belongs. You will receive one point for each set of three correct answers in a straight line and/or one correct answer in each of the four corners.

| | | |
|---|---|---|
| A | Ben & Jerry's | G | Haagen-Dazs | M | McDonnell Douglas |
| B | Boeing | H | IBM | N | NASA |
| C | Coca Cola | I | K Mart | O | Nike |
| D | Cray Research, Inc. | J | Kentucky Fried Chicken | P | Seagram & Sons, Inc. |
| E | French's Co. | K | McCormick & Co. | Q | U.S. Air Force |
| F | General Electric | L | McDonald's | R | Wal-Mart |

| To make, distribute, and sell the finest quality all-natural ice cream and related products in a wide variety of innovative flavors made from Vermont dairy products.<br><br>_____ | The company's mission is to lead in the development and marketing of supercomputers--<br><br>_____ | To satisfy the world's appetite for good food, well-served, at a price people can afford.<br><br>_____ |
|---|---|---|
| To defend the United States through control and exploitation of air and space.<br><br>_____ | The primary mission of _____ is to expand its worldwide leadership position in the spice, seasoning, and flavoring markets.<br><br>_____ | _____ will be a symbol to Americans--the place which helps them to attain the quality of life guaranteed in the American dream--sooner, better, and more conveniently than anyone else.<br><br>_____ |
| Our long-range mission is to be the number-one aerospace company in the world, and among the premier industrial firms, as measured by quality, profitability, and growth.<br><br>_____ | Boundaryless.....Speed.....Stretch<br><br>_____ | The mission of _____ is to be the best-managed beverage company in the world.<br><br>_____ |

# RESISTER BLISTERS

| | |
|---|---|
| **TOPIC** | Resistance to change |

Individuals resist change for a variety of reasons. Signs of resistance may become apparent when a company charts a new course and makes that new course known through a new vision statement. Workers may refuse to buy into the new vision because they feel threatened or because they were not given the opportunity to provide input.

**LEARNING OBJECTIVE**

Participants will be able to give some of the common reasons workers resist change.

**NUMBER OF PARTICIPANTS**

Any number

**PLAYING TIME**

12-15 minutes

**REQUIRED MATERIALS**

A set of Resister Blister Cards for each player and a copy of the Resister Blister Case Studies

**TO PLAY**

1. Introduce players to some of the reasons employees resist buying into new company visions in the workplace.
2. Go over the learning objective for the game.
3. Explain to players that they are going to pretend that a certain new vision will be implemented at their place of employment. They are next going to determine why they might resist the said vision, and they will cluster with other persons resisting the vision for the same reason.
4. Pass out a deck of Resister Blister Cards to each player.
5. Read Case Study #1.
6. Ask players to think of a reason they might resist the vision represented in the case study if a similar vision were to be implemented at their place of employment.
7. Direct players to read through their six Resister Blister Cards and pull out the card (only one card) which comes the closest to their main reason for resisting.

8. Advise players that they now have 30 seconds to form "resister blisters" (i.e., groups of individuals holding the identical Resister Blister Card).
9. After 30 seconds call "Stop" and identify the resister blister group with the most members. Verify that each person in the group is indeed holding the same Resister Blister Card.
10. Award each person in the largest resister blister group one point.
11 Ask participants to return to their original seats and place the Resister Blister Card back into their decks.
12. Repeat steps 5 through 11 for the remaining two case studies.
13. At the end of three rounds have players add up their scores (three is the highest possible score) and declare those with the most points, winners.
14 Debrief players. Discuss the Resister Blister Cards which seemed to be pulled from decks the most frequently (i.e., most common reasons for resistance). Identify ways these reasons for resistance can be constructively addressed by leaders. Have players share incidents when "resister blisters" appeared on a large scale in their organization.

**VARIATION**

Divide participants into small groups. Have each group write a vision case study profiling a recently proposed change in their organization. Collect all of the cases and ask players to stand. Explain that as you read a case study, they may sit down at any time they feel they can no longer go along with what is being proposed (i.e., when they feel like resisting). Count the number of players who remain standing at the end of each case study. Declare the vision encountering the least resistance the best case study and its authors winners.

**FOR MORE INFORMATION**

Fossum, L. (1989). *Understanding organizational change.* Menlo Park, CA: Crisp Publications, Inc.

# Resister Blister Case Studies

## Vision Case #1

You are currently a salesperson on commission at Yummy Snack Foods Company. In the present times of a health conscious public, sales are slipping, but not drastically so. Salespeople visit customers each week to take orders and handle complaints. Increased competition is coming from many both new and existing companies striving to produce and market healthy snacks. In reaction to declining sales, several new people have been hired into top management positions. Their vision for the furture of Yummy Snack Foods is as follows:

Yummy Snack Foods is #1 in healthy nutritious snacks. A new line of fruit and vegetable drinks is very profitable. Bakeries making the products have been relocated to areas of the country where labor is cheaper and taxes are much lower. Wholesale dealers take orders and supply the products to individual stores. Representatives from the company visit stores periodically to set up sales promotions and displays within the stores. Employees are well rewarded not only for coming up with new product ideas, but also for finding shortcuts and cost-saving measures for the manufacture and delivery of products.

## Vision Case #2

The Galaxy Motor Company has held a 20% market share of luxury cars sold in the country for the past 15 years. You have worked on the assembly line for all of those years. The emphasis of the company has always been on a quality 100% American-made product. All workers have been extensively trained in their areas of expertise. However, costs of materials and labor have increased steadily over the years. Government dealings with foreign countries have allowed competition from imports to skyrocket. If Galaxy is to remain in business, it must change drastically. The CEO and board of directors have created a new vision for bringing Galaxy into the next century.

Galaxy Motor Company will have increased its domestic market share to 35%. Streamlined operations will have increased profits by 25%. The company will have closed four of its older, less productive plants and automated production lines in the remaining five assembly plants. Many parts and subassemblies will be contracted out at much lower costs to companies in Japan, Korea, and Mexico. Galaxy's luxury cars will be sold in many foreign markets including the oil-rich nations of the Middle East. With the elevation in world presence of the Galaxy Motor Company will come an increase in status for owners of Galaxy automobiles. This in turn will allow the company to substantially raise prices of their cars with no detriment to the number of vehicles sold.

**Vision Case #3**

The Ding A Ling Phone Company has served a medium-sized rural area in the South for the past 40 years. Over the past eighteen years, you have worked your way up to the job of office supervisor. Last month, the board of directors announced that changes would be made concerning the future of Ding A Ling Phone. Citing the costs of keeping up with technology, the difficulty and cost involved in maintaining lines and equipment over a wide area with the present small crew of employees, and the demand for ever-increasing services from customers, the Board has developed a new vision for the direction of the company.

Five years in the future, Ding A Ling Phone will be a subsidiary of Busy Wires Phone Company, which serves the large cities in the three-state area. Customers will be efficiently served with well-maintained underground phone lines and the latest technology, supplying every available service. All employees will be highly trained via classes taught on a regular basis in the training facilty of Busy Wire. Linespeople and other outside workers will be dispatched from the central office located in the closest large city. An office staffed by a smaller workforce will remain in one of the small towns central to the rural area served.

## Resister Blister Cards

    To prepare a set of Resister Blister Cards, photocopy the following items on card-stock paper and cut them out.

| | |
|---|---|
| The vision is contrary to my personal values. | The vision is a new high in company greed. |
| I am likely to end up on the "short end" if the vision is implemented. | I do not trust the people proposing the vision. |
| If they wanted me to support this vision, they should have asked for my input. | The vision being proposed simply isn't workable. |

# VISION TELLING

TOPIC

Communicating a vision

Visioning can be thought of as a collaborative process whereby a group of individuals strive to clearly identify the desired future state of a company. It is one of the critical steps a company or department takes in constructing a strategic plan. For a vision to be realized, it is important that the vision be communicated to every employee in the organization.

LEARNING
OBJECTIVE

Participants will be able to define, create, and communicate a vision.

NUMBER OF
PARTICIPANTS

17 to 38 players divided into groups of 7 players and a crew of vision tellers

PLAYING TIME

15-30 minutes, depending upon the number of players

REQUIRED
MATERIALS

Vision Panels, medium-point blue or black markers for each group of players, a roll of masking tape, flip chart, and markers

TO PLAY

1. Introduce players to the concept of visioning.
2. Go over the learning objective for the game.
3. Explain to players that they are going to play a game which requires them to (1) create a vision, (2) draw picture elements which relate to the vision, (3) paste up the picture elements so as to form a vision collage.
4. Advise participants that each team of contestants will have two minutes to communicate their vision to a crew of vision tellers. If the vision tellers guess their vision correctly, the team receives one point. Teams receive one additional point for each picture element (panel) not used during the vision telling session. The team(s) earning the most points will be declared winners.
5. Select a crew of three vision tellers from the audience.
6. Divide the remaining participants into groups of seven players.

7. Tell each group that they have five minutes to come up with a company vision. Examples of company visions might include "to secure 80% of the market share in a particular industry, to be a winner of the Malcolm Baldrige Award, to achieve a 99% customer service rating."

8. Pass out the Vision Panels and at least four markers to each group. Explain that every member of the group is to now draw a picture of a person, place, thing, or symbol on one of the seven vision panels. Make sure that participants understand that only one image can appear on a single panel and that no written words can be used.

9. Explain that when placed alongside one another, the group's panels should form a complete panoramic image of the vision they are attempting to convey to the crew of vision tellers.

10. Give members five minutes to draw their vision panels. While the group may collaborate on the nature of the images to be drawn on the various panels, each member must personally create one drawing.

11. After five minutes call one group of contestants and the crew of vision tellers to the front of the room. Have one member of the group whisper its vision to you, making certain that it is not audible to any of the vision tellers.

12. Hand a roll of masking tape to the group. Explain that they have two minutes to paste up their individual vision panels in such a way as to communicate their vision to the crew of vision tellers. The panels may be taped to the wall in any order and as rapidly or as slowly as the group desires. While, as in the game of charades, they can gesture, point, and nod their heads yes or no, they are not allowed to speak to anyone during their vision presentation. If they do speak to one another, to one of the panel members, or to someone in the audience, they are immediately disqualified.

13. Remind players that they receive one point if the panel guesses their vision and one additional bonus point for each vision panel not posted before the panel guesses the correct vision.

14. Inform panel members that they are to individually or collectively call out visions they believe the contestants are attempting to communicate. In return, contestants may respond with gestures indicating the correctness of the guesses.

15. Have the first group present their vision. Record the number of points earned.
16. Have the remaining groups present their visions and record the points earned.
17. Declare the group(s) with the most points winners and true visionaries.
18. Debrief players. Ask participants to decide which is a more difficult task, to forge a collective vision or to communicate a vision to others. Using one simple sentence, have players give their company's vision. List and discuss some   common themes running through the vision statements.

**VARIATION**

Select a crew of three vision tellers. Have all other participants individually create one vision panel according to the above directions. Collect, shuffle, and deal the entire set of panels to the three vision tellers. Have each vision teller select six panels from their stack and tape them to the wall with masking tape. Each set of panels should present a panoramic view of a company's potential vision. Ask players in the audience to vote on the vision they like best. Declare the vision teller and panel contributors associated with the best-liked vision, winners.

**FOR MORE INFORMATION**

Goman, C. (1991). *Managing for commitment.* Menlo Park, CA: Crisp Publications, Inc.
Heim, P. & Chapman, E. (1990). *Learning to lead.* Menlo Park, CA: Crisp Publications, Inc.

## Vision  Panels

To prepare a set of Vision Panels, make seven copies of the following item on card-stock paper and cut them out.

# VISION TESTING 1,2,3

**TOPIC**  Support for visions

A vision is an imaged state of a company's future. Most leaders agree that a vision has a better chance of becoming reality if it enjoys wide support throughout the organization. Therefore a leader or leadership team may want to test the support employees are willing to give a particular vision before making it the company's official vision.

**LEARNING OBJECTIVE**  Participants will be able to test support for a proposed vision.

**NUMBER OF PARTICIPANTS**  Any number

**PLAYING TIME**  20-30 minutes

**REQUIRED MATERIALS**  A copy of Multimillions Media's Vision Statement, pencils, paper, flip chart, and markers

**TO PLAY**
1. Introduce players to the concept of vision testing.
2. Go over the learning objective for the game.
3. Advise players that they are going to be divided into small groups to create short vision statements for an imaginary company.
4. Explain that their visions will then be tested. The group that comes up with a vision receiving the most support becomes the winner.
5. Tell participants that they will first test a sample vision to see how the game is played.
6. Ask all participants to stand.
7. Inform players that you will now read aloud a vision statement. Advise them that they are to sit down whenever anything is read that they can't personally support. Ask them to attempt to remember at what point (i.e., number) in the vision they sat down.
8. Slowly read Multimillions Media's Vision Statement.
9. Count the number of individuals standing at the end of the reading. Attempt to identify the points in the statement where the greatest number of players

sat down. Discuss what this information means in terms of support for Multimillions Media's Vision Statement.
10. Divide participants into groups of five players.
11. Supply each group with a pencil and two or three sheets of paper.
12. Direct each group to write a brief vision statement (i.e., no more than 10 points) for an imaginary company. Each key part of the vision should be numbered.
13. After 10 minutes collect the vision statements.
14. Following steps six through nine above, read each group's vision statement.
15. Declare the group with the most players standing after the reading of their vision statement, the winner.
16. Debrief players. Discuss what it was about the winning vision statement that enabled so many participants to support it. Identify common themes among the visions' various sticking points (i.e., parts of visions players failed to support). List on a flip chart other ways companies or departments might test their vision statements.

**VARIATION**

Instead of writing visions during the game, use actual vision statements from within the company. Try not to give away the identity of the department in reading the vision statement (i.e., substitute a fictitious name for the name of the department). Declare the department whose vision gets the most support the winning department. Otherwise, play the game according to the above rules.

**FOR MORE INFORMATION**

Goman, C. (1991). *Managing for commitment.* Menlo Park, CA: Crisp Publications, Inc.
Heim, P. & Chapman, E. (1990). *Learning to lead.* Menlo Park, CA: Crisp Publications, Inc.

## Multimillions Media's Vision Statement

1. In five years, Multimillions Media will look more like multibillions because it will be the largest, most diversified media conglomerate in the world. 2. Dividends to stockholders will have tripled. 3. Through the acquisition of a large publisher, a television news network, and a worldwide computer network added to an already powerful motion picture, radio, and television entertainment empire, Multimillions will serve the world community. 4. A CEO will preside over a board of directors made up of the largest stockholders and the presidents of each division of the organization. 5. A highly diverse workforce made up of male and female employees of all cultural backgrounds and age groups will provide the highest quality products and services possible. 6. Each division, though cooperating fully with each other, will be responsible for separate parts of the organization (i.e., motion pictures, radio, television news, television entertainment, print media, computer networking, and worldwide communications). 7. Each division will be directed by a president, with vicepresidents for each subdivision and managers supervising work teams at all levels. 8. Employees will participate in the decision-making process through the use of employee advisory groups. 9. Promotions will be internal whenever possible, with ability, longevity, commitment to the organization, and recommendation of superiors as factors in the promotion process. 10. Employees will display the highest level of ethical behavior, and they will refrain from leaking information to competitors as this will result in immediate dismissal and possible legal prosecution.

11. Promising young employees, both male and female, will be groomed to assume management positions to ensure the continuity of excellence. 12. Outplacement assistance and compensation for those laid off or dismissed will be commensurate with the worker's level of employment in the organization. 13. Employees will be offered the option of purchasing company stock as part of a profit-sharing and retirement package. Gifts of stock shares will be given to employees as bonuses on their 10 year anniversaries and every 5 years thereafter.

14. Productivity, quality, and creativity will be highly rewarded with bonuses, vacations, stock, and other incentives. 15. Multimillions will support the family structure of its employees by providing on-site day care centers, flextime and work-at-home programs for some workers, and unpaid leaves of absence for mothers or fathers wishing to be at home with a new baby for up to six months. 16. Multimillions will be a true equal-opportunity organization in hiring and promoting employees regardless of sex, age, race, ethnic background, or sexual orientation. 17. Employee development will be emphasized for all employees through training programs and educational reimbursement. All employees must participate in at least 160 hours of training per year, half of which will be on the employees' own time. 18. Health care will be supported by offering employees choices in health care insurance programs. An on-site fitness facility will be provided,

and use of tobacco, alcohol, or drugs on the job will not be tolerated. Employees who smoke will be required to pay a 20% surcharge on health insurance coverage. Counseling for alcohol and/or drug addiction is mandatory for continued employment.

19. Safety will be the responsibility of every employee. Violation of a safety regulation will be reprimanded and more than three violations in a six-month period will result in a fine or dismissal depending on the severity of the infraction. 20. Multimillions, as a major employer and presence in the community, will be involved on a grand scale in service to the community. Not only will the organization financially contribute to community projects, but every employee will be required to participate in a community service endeavor on a continuous basis.

# Chapter Six

# Hybrid Learning Games

# BLIND REFLECTIONS

**TOPIC**

Active listening and reflecting

Reflecting refers to a communication feedback technique whereby a listener feeds back to a speaker what she or he believes the speaker has just said. The listener may begin such feedback with "You're saying" or "You feel." These words are followed by the listener paraphrasing what the speaker has communicated. The listener then pauses to allow the speaker to verify the accuracy of the reflection. The speaker may say "Yes," nod her or his head in agreement with the interpretation, or clarify any perceived misunderstanding on the part of the listener. The purpose of the feedback is to assure that clear communication is taking place.

**LEARNING OBJECTIVE**

Participants will be able to reflect in their own words comments made by others.

**NUMBER OF PARTICIPANTS**

Any number divided into groups of 5 players

**PLAYING TIME**

12-15 minutes

**REQUIRED MATERIALS**

A copy of the Client Problems Sheets for each client, flip chart, and markers

**TO PLAY**

1. Introduce players to the skill of active listening and reflecting.
2. Go over the learning objective for the game.
3. Explain to players that they are going to play a short game which requires certain participants to engage in active listening and reflecting.
4. Divide the larger group into teams of five players. Team members need to know one another, but they should not be close friends.
5. Ask each group to select a "client." With her or his back turned to the other members of the group, the "client" will attempt to identify players as they reflect her/his comments.
6. Advise the other four members of the group that they will play the role of reflectors. With the client looking in the other direction, they will take turns

accurately reflecting their client's comments (i.e., paraphrasing what the client has just said). They will preface their comments with such phrases as "I hear you saying..." or "I think you're feeling...."

7. Tell clients that their job is to be the first client in the room to guess the names of all four of their reflectors.

8. Inform the reflectors that their goal is to be the last person in their group to be identified by their client. To prevent being identified reflectors may need to disguise their voices by holding their noses, putting their hands in front of mouths, or talking in a falsetto voice.

9. Pass out a copy of the Client Problems Sheet to each client.

10. Direct the client in each group to sit with her or his back to the reflectors. Remind clients that at no time during the game are they to turn around and face their reflectors.

11. Ask reflectors to form a line in random order three feet behind their group's client.

12. Explain that play begins with the client reading the first problem item on her or his Client Problems Sheet. The first reflector, in a disguised voice, is to reflect what the client has said. The client may then attempt to guess the reflector's name. If successful, the reflector acknowledges that she/he has been correctly identified and leaves the game. Play continues with the client reading another item from the Client Problems Sheet and the next reflector in line making a reflection and so on. If the client is unsuccessful in guessing the name of a reflector, the client repeats the same problem and next person in line makes a reflective response. Play continues until the client has identified all four reflectors.

13. Direct clients to yell out "Blind reflection" when they have successfully identified all the reflectors in their group.

14. Call "Begin."

15. As soon as each group has completed a round of play, have the client who finished first stand and declare her or him the "winning client."

16. Have all the winning reflectors in the groups stand and declare them "winning reflectors."

17. Debrief players. Ask participants to describe the person in their department with the best active listening skills. On flip chart, list ways people might improve their active listening. Discuss

whether it is more important to be able to reflect people's ideas or feelings. Ask players to explain their answers.

**VARIATION**    Have players write down five sentences on a three-by-five index card. Each sentence should consist of a message they would like their company or someone in their company to understand. Divide the audience into pairs. Seat the pairs on chairs back-to-back. Taking turns, players should read one of their statements aloud. Without turning around, the partners should reflect in their own words what they believe they have heard. Items which have been reflected back correctly should be checked. The person having correctly reflected back the most statements becomes the winner of the match.

**FOR MORE INFORMATION**    Egan, G. (1994) *The skilled helper*. (5th ed.). Pacific Grove, CA: Brooks/Cole.


## Client Problems Sheets


1. My boss stinks.
2. I don't have a key to the executive washroom.
3. There are personality conflicts in my work team.
4. Our new product line is cheap.
5. My company's benefits package is "Third World."
6. The money's good, but the job sucks!
7. I want more responsibility.
8. Upper management never listens to us peons.
9. My boss plays favorites.
10. My coworkers gossip too much.
11. My job is making me sick.
12. I should have been promoted by now.
13. One of my coworkers is a back-stabber.
14. Management in this company is strictly "Stone Age."
15. The corporate ladder in this company has slippery rungs.
16. Doing my job is like fighting a high-tech war with a Civil War musket.
17. The boss uses my ideas to make herself or himself look good.
18. Our CEO can't see outside her or his mirrored office.
19. Our company's suggestion box is just for decoration.
20. My boss blames me for his problem.

# BODY LISTENING

| | |
|---|---|
| **TOPIC** | Body language |

Individuals communicate not only through spoken words, but also through movements of their body and gestures. The study of what particular facial expressions, gestures, body postures, and body movements communicate to others is known as the science of kinesics. Communication experts estimate that 7 percent of one's communication is the choice of words spoken, 38 percent is the voice tone used in speaking, and 55 percent is body language. Therefore, some understanding of kinesics is essential for team members to communicate effectively with one another.

**LEARNING OBJECTIVE**

Participants will be able to discern what others are communicating through various facial expressions, gestures, postures, and body movements.

**NUMBER OF PARTICIPANTS**

6 to 30 players

**PLAYING TIME**

12-15 minutes

**REQUIRED MATERIALS**

Slips of paper containing various body movements to be acted out, flip chart, and markers

**TO PLAY**

1. Introduce players to the concept of body listening (i.e., listening to what people are communicating by way of their body language).
2. Go over the learning objective for the game.
3. Explain to players that they are about to be given a slip of paper containing a body movement to be acted out. If they wish, they will have the opportunity to come forward and demonstrate the body movement to the rest of the audience. If the audience guesses the meaning of the body movement within 30 seconds, they receive a point. Answers must reflect the meaning of the message but need not be the exact words appearing on the Body Language Slips. The facilitator is the final judge as to the correctness of any answer.
4. Pass slips of paper containing descriptions of body movements and their meaning to each player. Each

player should receive a different body movement to perform. They are not to tell anyone else the contents of their slips of paper.

5. After participants have had the opportunity to read the body movement on their slips of paper, ask for a volunteer to come forward and demonstrate her or his body movement.

6. Advise players that they cannot speak a word. They are only to demonstrate the body movement. Furthermore, they should take care to demonstrate only one body movement. Multiple body movements may confuse the audience.

7. Inform players that they can demonstrate the body movement as many times as they like. They can also exaggerate the movement for demonstration purposes.

8. Explain to players that they may call on anyone in the audience to guess the meaning of their body movement. However, members in the audience must be called upon before offering an interpretation of the body movement. If they guess the communication message correctly, they receive a point.

9. Give the first player 30 seconds to demonstrate and have the audience guess the body movement on their slip of paper.

10. Repeat step eight as many times as the number of slips of paper or time permits.

11. Ask any player who earned two points during the game to stand and be recognized as a winner and excellent "body listener."

12. Debrief players. Ask participants what they pay most attention to when listening to a colleague at work: the words they speak, the voice tone being used, or the body movements accompanying the spoken words. Identify participants in the audience who are willing to admit that they closely monitor their own body language. Have them discuss why and how they go about such self-monitoring. On a flip chart, list other body movements and their meanings not included on the slips of paper. Discuss with what frequency such movements are used by colleagues.

**VARIATION**    Play the game according to the above directions, but this time have a select panel from the audience guess the message of the body movements appearing on the slips of paper. The audience could first be divided into three groups which, in turn, could select one of its own members to serve on the panel. The panel member (as well as the team she or he represents) making the most correct guesses would become the winner. Each panel member would get two chances to come up with a correct answer.

**FOR MORE INFORMATION**

McGough, E. (1974). *Your silent language.* New York: William Morrow and Company.
Nierenberg, G. I. & Calero, H. H. (1971). *How to read a person like a book.* New York: Hawthorn Books, Inc.

## Body Movement Slips

To prepare a set of Body Movement Slips, duplicate the following items and cut out each individual item.

1. Embarrassment: Rub your face with your hand.

2. Dejection: Walk across the room with your shoulders slumped forward, head bent, and hands hanging at your sides.

3. Honesty: Hold your hands spread out with palms up in front of you.

4. Defensiveness: Hold your arms crossed over your chest with hands gripping the upper part of the opposite arm.

5. Boredom: Sit on a chair with legs crossed: Make a slight kicking movement with the top foot.

6. Thinking or evaluating: Stroke your chin.

7. Suspicion: Stand with your feet apart, thumbs hooked in your waistband, and a slight frown on your face.

8. Doubt: Lightly touch the side of your nose with your index finger.

9. Ready to go: Stand with your right foot a little forward and your hands on your hips.

10. Frustration: Bend your head slightly down and scratch the back of it.

11. In a bind or on the "hot seat:" Wring your hands in front of you.

12. Irritation with someone or something: Place the palm of your hand on the back of your neck.

13. Confidence: Stand straight with tips of fingers on left hand pressed against those of your right hand in a steeple position.

14. Authority: Stand straight, hold your hands behind your back, and raise your chin.

15. Superiority: Sit on a chair with legs leisurely crossed and hands joined at the back of your head supporting it.

16. Astonishment: Open your eyes wide and cover your mouth with your hand.

17. Disgust: Wrinkle your nose and raise your upper lip and cheeks in a grimace.

18. Defiance: Tighten your lips and jaws, narrow your eyes, and stick out your chin.

19. Hello: Look the audience in the eye and pleasantly smile, showing only your upper teeth.

20. Disapproval: Frown and shake your head from side to side.

21. Stressed Out: Sit stiffly in a chair with your hands clenched in your lap.

22. Expectation: Rub your hands in front of you in anticipation of a treat.

23. Upset/tense: Pace back and forth, then sit down on a chair for a moment. Stand up and resume pacing.

24. Disinterest: Stand with your shoulder turned away from the audience, looking elsewhere.

25. What do you want from me?: Shrug your shoulders and hold your hands out, palms up, in front of you.

26. A tough decision: Close your eyes and pinch the bridge of your nose.

27. Need reassurance: Stick a pen or pencil in your mouth and chew or suck on it.

28. Hoping for good luck: Raise your hand and cross your fingers.

29. Shyness: Peek at the audience and then turn your eyes away while smiling and drawing in your bottom lip.

30. Everything will be OK: Go to someone in the audience and pat him or her on the arm or hand.

# DOMINO COMMUNICO

**TOPIC**

Communication climate

At the heart of a learning organization is a free and honest dialogue. It is through the exchange of ideas and feelings that new understandings are gained, mental models revised, visions conveyed, and group consensus reached. However, a free and candid dialogue requires an organization climate that nurtures open communication between all parties.

**LEARNING OBJECTIVE**

Participants will be able to construct a favorable communication environment.

**NUMBER OF PARTICIPANTS**

Any number of players divided into groups of four

**PLAYING TIME**

15-18 minutes

**REQUIRED MATERIALS**

A set of Communications Dominos for each small group of players, flip chart, and markers

**TO PLAY**

1. Introduce players to the concept of communication climate.
2. Go over the learning objective for the game.
3. Inform participants that they will be divided into small teams to compete with one another in the construction of a good communication climate. The object of the game is to be the first group to complete a communication environment.
4. Explain that each team will be given a set of Communications Dominos from which to construct a four-by-four domino (total of 16 dominos) communication environment. Except for the blanks, each domino contains a condition which makes for good communication in the workplace. Blanks contain undesirable communication conditions.
5. Divide participants into groups of four players. Each group should form a circle around a table or on the floor if they so desire.
6. Provide each group a set of Communications Dominos.

7.  Have someone in each group remove the double-blank domino and thoroughly shuffle the rest of the stack.
8.  Request that each group place their set of dominos facedown in the center of the group. Ask them to place the double-six domino faceup, thus beginning the construction of their communication environment.
9.  Explain that play is to proceed clockwise around the group with each player taking turns at drawing a domino from the top of the draw pile. They are to attempt to match the drawn domino with a domino at either end of their partially completed four-by-four domino communication environment.
10. Advise players that if a match occurs, the player is to read the communication condition written on the matching end of the drawn domino, give a concrete example of the condition, and place the domino faceup next to the matching end. If the domino doesn't match either end of the partially completed communication environment, a player is to return it to the bottom of the domino draw pile and draw another domino until a match is found.
11. Tell players that whenever blank ends constitute a match, a player must give a condition which might contribute to a poor communication environment. Furthermore, she or he is required to call on another player to give another concrete example of a poor communication condition.
12. Inform participants that as soon as any group has successfully constructed their four-by-four domino communication environment they are to call out "Domino Communico."
13. As soon as a group calls out "Domino Communico" have them stand to be recognized as the winners.
14. Debrief players. Ask participants to identify the two most important conditions for a good communication environment. Have them list ways a better communication environment might be achieved within their own immediate work groups.

**VARIATION**    Play the game with real dominos. Prior to starting the game have participants list six conditions of a good communication environment in the workplace on a flip chart. As dominos are placed in the game, players are required to give an example of the matching domino number's condition on the flip chart. For example, if a four on a domino is butted up against another four, the player gives an example of number four on the flip chart. Blank places on dominos would not require any examples.

**FOR MORE INFORMATION**

Conlow, R. (1991). *Excellence in management.* Menlo Park, CA: Crisp Publications, Inc.

## Communications Dominos

To prepare a set of Communications Dominos, photocopy the following items on card-stock paper and cut them out.

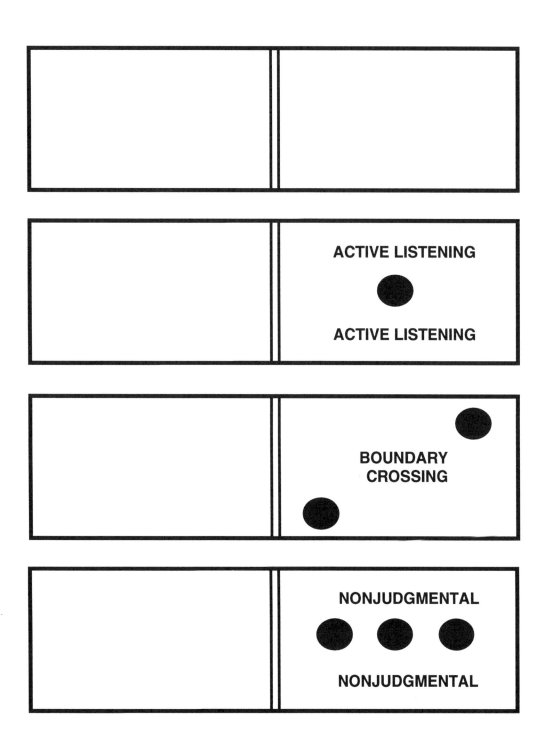

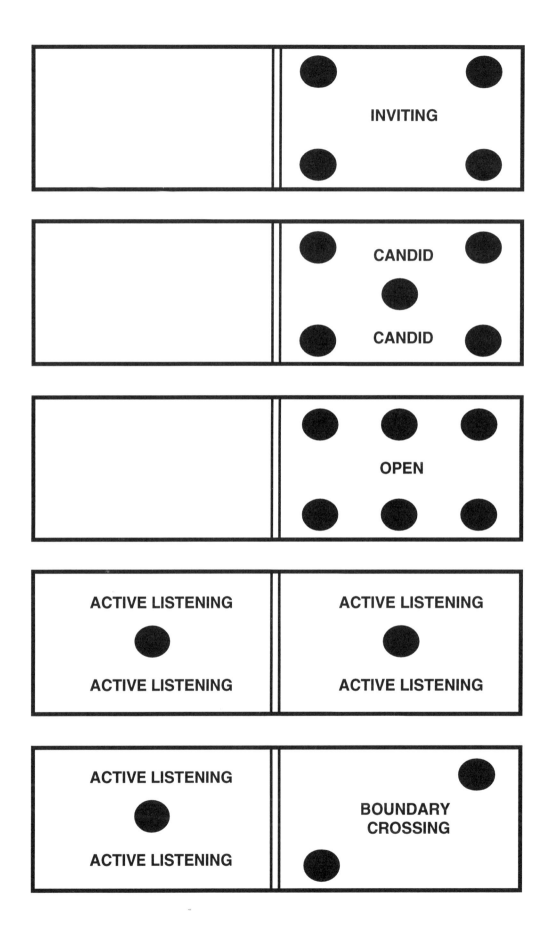

235

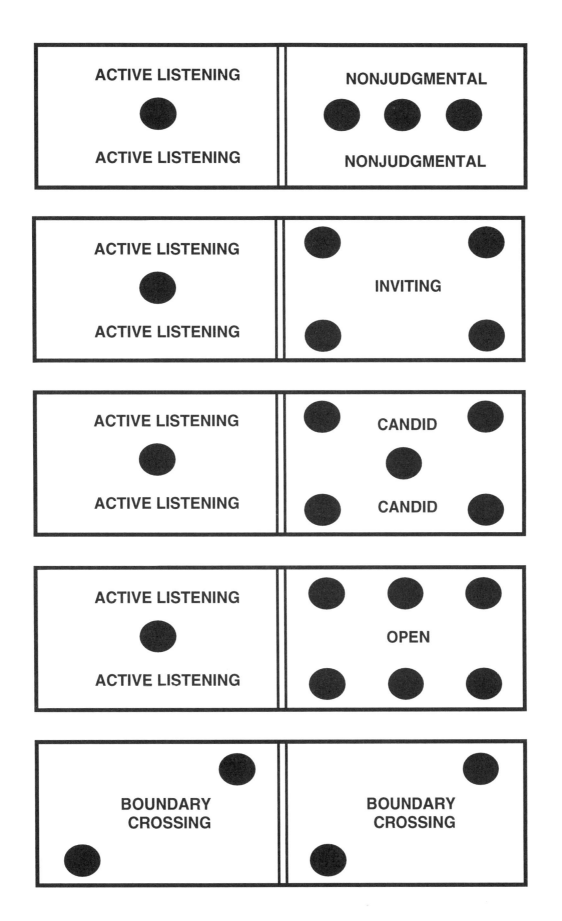

236

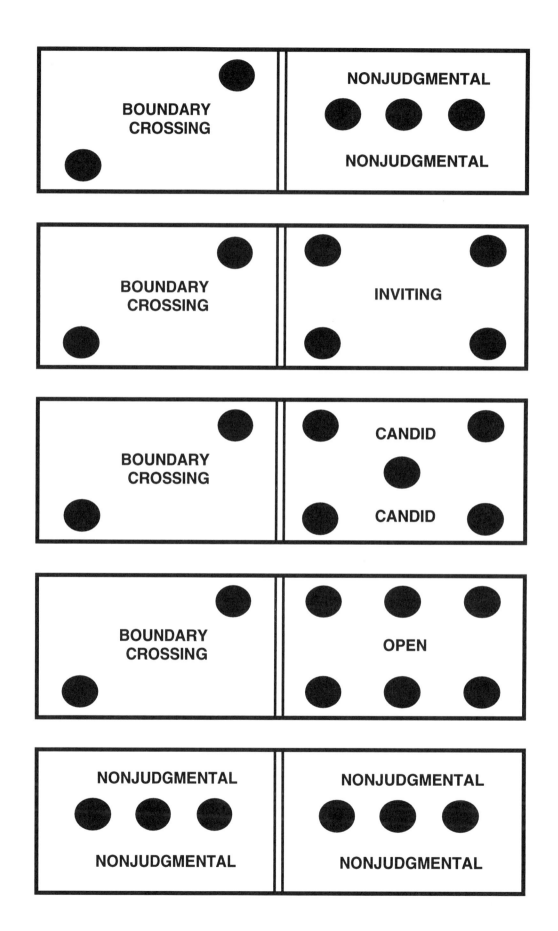

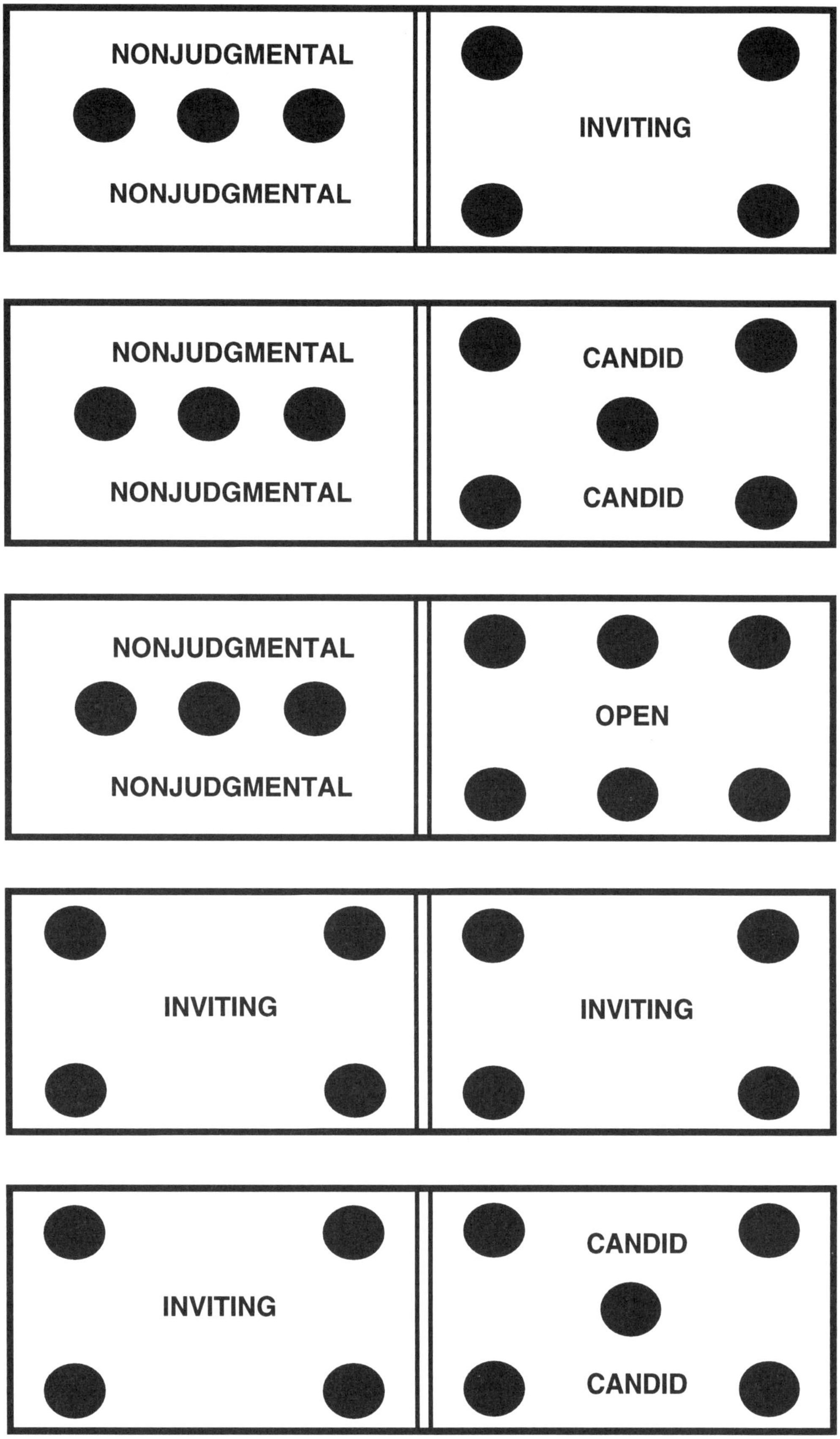
NONJUDGMENTAL
NONJUDGMENTAL
INVITING
NONJUDGMENTAL
NONJUDGMENTAL
CANDID
CANDID
NONJUDGMENTAL
NONJUDGMENTAL
OPEN
INVITING
INVITING
INVITING
CANDID
CANDID

238

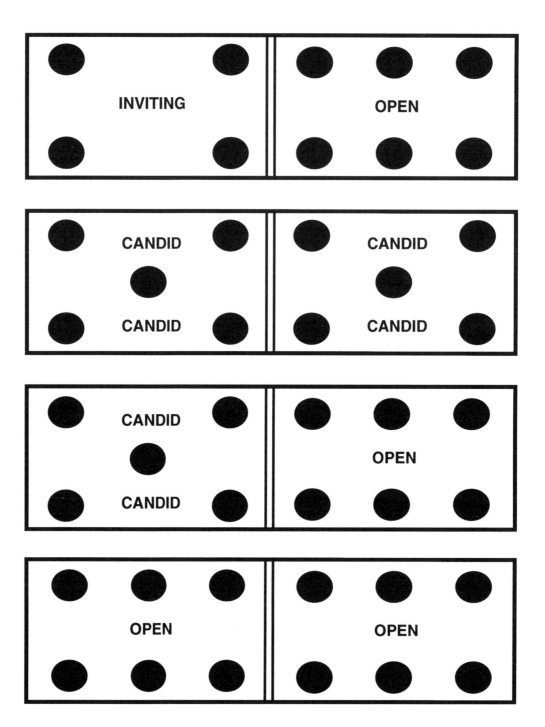

# JIGSAW

**TOPIC**   Jigsaw cooperative learning technique

The Jigsaw group learning technique calls for a topic or body of information to be divided into parts or subtopics. In addition to becoming generally familiar with the overall topic, each group member must become an expert on one of the subtopics (i.e., pieces of the information puzzle). They are then given the responsibility of teaching their assigned area of expertise to all members of their group. The goal is for the entire group to master the subject at hand.

**LEARNING OBJECTIVE**   Participants will be able to use the jigsaw cooperative learning technique to facilitate team learning.

**NUMBER OF PARTICIPANTS**   Any number divided into groups of five players each

**PLAYING TIME**   15-30 minutes

**REQUIRED MATERIALS**   Copies of the poem, Goals, pencils, blank sheets of paper, flip chart, and markers

**TO PLAY**
1. Introduce players to the cooperative learning technique known as "jigsaw learning."
2. Go over the learning objective for the game.
3. Explain to participants that they will be divided into groups of five to learn the poem "Goals."
4. Inform players that they must use the jigsaw learning technique to teach each other the poem "Goals." The first group to have all members learn the poem will be declared the winning team.
5. Divide the large group into teams of five players.
6. Pass out copies of the poem and pencils to each player.
7. Ask players to generally familiarize themselves with the poem by reading through it one time.
8. Have each team decide which member will teach the group the respective five stanzas.
9. Give players sufficient time to memorize their particular stanzas and plan how they will teach their stanza to other team members.

10. Allow groups a sufficient amount of time to learn the poem, "Goals." Explain that when they believe all team members know the poem by heart, they are to call "Jigsaw."

11. When a team has called "Jigsaw," pass each team member a blank sheet of paper to write down the poem from memory.

12. If each member of the group who called "jigsaw" writes the poem correctly without any help from teammates, the group becomes the winner of the game. If any of the members fail to write the poem correctly (spelling not counted), the team is disqualified and play continues until a winner is found.

13. Debrief players. Ask players' opinions as to whether they think the jigsaw technique enabled them to learn the poem "Goals" more quickly than they might have otherwise learned it. Discuss the advantages and disadvantages of the jigsaw group learning technique. List the types of information that might best be learned using the jigsaw method. Have participants give instances in which they might use the jigsaw learning technique.

**VARIATION**      Divide the larger groups into teams of four players and have them learn only one paragraph of the poem "Goals," or select some other information you would like the group to try learning using the jigsaw method described above.

**FOR MORE INFORMATION**

Slavin, R. E. (1983). *Cooperative learning*. New York: Longman.
Slavin, R. E. (1988). *Student team learning: An overview and practical guide*. Washington, D.C.: National Education Association of the United States.

# Goals

To be the best that you can be,
It's your inner self that you must see.
When your intrinsic desires are truly clear,
You can accomplish what you hold dear.

There are many truths you will find.
But faulty thinking may clutter your mind.
A healthy cleanup of this debris
Will open your eyes and set you free.

A ship without water won't be able to float.
The winter is cold if you haven't a coat.
Thus to accomplish your vision, you have to share
Your ideas with others who'll support you and care.

You must assemble a good team to meet your goal,
For each person involved will fill a big role.
You'll learn from each other what you need to know.
From collaborative thinking great ideas will flow.

Each person or group must do their bit.
Into a grand scheme, each piece will fit.
When all work together as parts of a whole,
It's much easier to accomplish a difficult goal.

L. Kirk

# QUESTION MY QUESTION

| | |
|---|---|
| TOPIC | Questioning |

Questions are requests for information. Asked effectively, questions can motivate learners to think and engage in lively discussion. Learners' responses to questions are affected by several factors including the type of question being asked. Closed-ended questions can usually be answered in one or two words, often by a simple "yes" or "no." For example, "Have you done any re-engineering at your firm?" On the other hand, open-ended questions typically require explanation or elaboration. For example, "How did your company go about re-engineering its process for handling customer complaints?" As a rule, open-ended questions are more effective for stimulating discussion.

**LEARNING OBJECTIVE**

Participants will be able to effectively ask open-ended questions.

**NUMBER OF PARTICIPANTS**

Any number

**PLAYING TIME**

15-30 minutes

**REQUIRED MATERIALS**

Pencils, paper, and set of practice questions

**TO PLAY**

1. Introduce participants to the concept of closed- and open-ended questions.
2. Go over the learning objective for the game.
3. Explain to players that they are going to be divided into groups of three to try their hands at rapidly asking both closed-ended and open-ended questions. Two people in each group will be questioners, and one person will serve as the moderator.
4. Tell participants that the moderator is responsible for selecting the topics of discussion, keeping time, recording scores, and resolving any disputes.
5. Inform participants that the object of the game is to quickly answer your partner's question with a question of your own. Furthermore, if your partner asks a closed-ended question, you must quickly respond with an open-ended question. If your

partner asks an open-ended question, you must quickly respond with an closed-ended question. The response question must relate to the topic of the original question. For example, if one partner says, "Do you like fish?" (closed-ended question), her or his partner might appropriately respond with "What kind of fish do you like?" (open-ended question). Response must be made in five seconds. If no appropriate response is made in five seconds, the responder does not receive a point and play continues with the original questioner asking another question.

6. Explain that the shortest partner goes first by asking six questions of her or his own creation (three open-ended and three closed-ended), with the other partner appropriately responding. Afterward the second partner gets to ask her or his six questions.

7. Advise players that each time they return an appropriate response, they receive a point. Thus the maximum points any player can earn is six points. The player in each pair who has the most points at the end of the game becomes the winner.

8. Before starting the game have two people come to the front to use the set of practice questions and have the facilitator serve as the moderator. Play a practice round.

9. Have participants divide into groups of three and decide who will be the moderator.

10. Pass out pencils and sheets of paper on which players are to write their questions (three open-ended and three closed-ended). Have moderators whisper a different topic in the ear of each contestant.

11. Give players five minutes to write down three closed-ended and three open-ended questions on the topic that was whispered by the moderator.

12. Direct players to begin.

13. After all groups have had the opportunity to play at least one round, ask the winners to stand and declare them "master questioners."

14. Debrief players. On a flip chart, list circumstances in which it is most appropriate to ask closed-ended questions and circumstances when it is most appropriate to ask open-ended questions. Discuss which type of question (open-ended vs. closed-ended) participants find more difficult to ask. Ask them to explain their answers. Have participants

suggest ways of improving open-ended questioning skills.

**VARIATION**     Play the game according to the above directions using prepared questions on flash cards. Flash cards might contain three open-ended and three closed-ended questions. All questions should relate to a topic of great interest to players.

**FOR MORE INFORMATION**     Egan, G. (1994) *The skilled helper.* (5th ed.). Pacific Grove, CA: Brook/Cole.

## Practice Questions

Topic: Office Equipment

1. Can you operate a high-speed copy machine? (closed-ended)
2. What spreadsheet programs do you have on your computer? (open-ended)
3. Where do you think the new file cabinet should go? (open-ended)
4. Is your printer out of toner? (closed-ended)
5. What are the features of the salesteam's new pagers? (open-ended)
6. Do you like our new voice mail system? (closed-ended)

Topic: Customer Service

1. How can we be more responsive to our clients needs? (open-ended)
2. Are your clients satisfied with our new overnight delivery carrier? (closed-ended)
3. How can our repair service be improved? (open-ended)
4. Did the Johnson Company get their order on time? (closed-ended)
5. Are you able to return phone calls from clients promptly? (closed-ended)
6. What are the strong points of our customer service department? (open-ended)

# SOUND OFF

| | |
|---|---|
| **TOPIC** | Male and female communications |

Men and women differ in their communication patterns. It is widely believed that both inherent and cultural factors account for many of these observed differences. In general, women are thought to be more intuitive, passive, questioning, indirect, and process-oriented in their communication patterns. Men are said to be more bottom-line-oriented, competitive, direct, aggressive, and linear in their communication.

**LEARNING OBJECTIVE**

Participants will be able to better communicate with members of the opposite sex.

**NUMBER OF PARTICIPANTS**

Any number divided into groups of five or seven players

**PLAYING TIME**

15-30 minutes, depending on the number of players

**REQUIRED MATERIALS**

A tennis or nerf ball for each group, a set of What They Said statements for each group facilitator, flip chart, and markers

**TO PLAY**

1. Introduce players to the concept of communication pattern differences between men and women.
2. Go over the learning objective for the game.
3. Explain to players that they are about to engage in some friendly competition between the sexes. After a selected statement is read aloud, team members will attempt to identify whether it is more commonly made by a male or a female. A point will be awarded for each correct answer. The teams that end the game with the highest number of correct answers will be declared winners.
4. Divide the audience into groups of five or seven persons (for audiences of 28 or more individuals, divide into groups of seven). Five-member groups should have either three males and two females or three females and two males. Seven-member groups should have either four males and three females or four females and three males.

5. Select a facilitator in each group. This person will direct the competitive play within the group. Choose a facilitator from the gender having the most individuals in a given group. One half of the remaining members should be female and the other half male. The female members will constitute a team competing against a team of male members.

6. Direct the members of each group to form a circle with an eight-foot diameter and with every other person being of the opposite gender. Groups should be spread about the room at least 10 feet apart.

7. Provide each group facilitator with a What They Said sheet of quotations and a tennis or nerf ball.

8. Ask facilitators to think of a number from 1 to 100. Have them ask members in their respective groups to give a number. Facilitators should hand the ball to the person giving a number closest to the one they had in mind. This contestant will have the opportunity to answer the first of 10 statements.

9. Explain that only the person holding the ball can guess the answer to a statement. If she or he answers correctly, her or his team (the male or female team within the group) receives a point. If the person does not answer the question correctly, the ball passes to the other team. After a statement has been answered correctly, the player then throws the ball to a teammate. If she or he catches the ball, she or he has the opportunity to answer the next statement. If for any reason she or he does not catch the ball, then the ball goes to a member of the opposing team. Opponents can attempt to block a throw of the ball, but they cannot move out of their positions in the circle nor can they shove an opponent.

10. Advise players that if all members of the opposing male and female teams agree on an answer different from the one on the What They Said sheet, it may be considered the correct answer.

11. Tell facilitators to begin the game by reading the first statement to the player with the ball. If the answer is correct, the facilitator is to record a point for the respective team and continue play.

12. After 10 statements have been read in each of the groups, declare the team with the most points the winner. Statements 11 and 12 may be used to break any ties which may occur.

13. Debrief players. Discuss any statements for which groups agreed to change the correct answer. Have them give their reasons for changing the answer.

Ask participants to identify the single most significant difference in communication between males and females. Discuss challenges this difference presents in the workplace. On flip chart, list communication patterns which make people particularly good leaders. Beside each item, identify the gender (M for male and F for female) which more frequently displays the pattern.

**VARIATION**

In place of the statements on the What They Said sheet, have participants write two phrases commonly used around the office on separate three-by-five index cards. Ask that they indicate whether they believe the phrase more closely represents the communication patterns of males or females. Collect the cards. Form small groups and select facilitators according to the above directions. Provide each facilitator with five of the index cards. Play the game according to the above rules, with the winning team being the team with the most points after the reading of five statements.

**FOR MORE INFORMATION**

Gray, J. (1992). *Men are from Mars, women are from Venus.* New York: Harper Collins.
Tannen, D. (1990). *You just don't understand: Women and men in conversation.* New York: Ballantine Books.

## What They Said

1. When the chairperson of the board of directors asked for comments on what consultant to hire, Chris said " I can't help but feel that the one from Acme would be our best choice." (F)

2. Standing with a group of coworkers at the company Christmas party, drink in hand, Dale says, "They couldn't have closed that deal in England without me."(M)

3. Drinking coffee with a close friend in the hospital cafeteria, Lee says, "We need lots more information about the medical options before we can make any decisions about Mom's treatment."(F)

4. When getting the runaround at the local department store from a harried salesclerk about returning a jacket, Lynn says, "I demand to speak to your supervisor immediately!" (M)

5. An observer, seeing Bobby searching for a particular office in a large complex, offers assistance and Bobby says, "Thanks, but I think I can find it myself." (M)

6. Sitting at the table in a department meeting called to discuss the marketing of a new type of snack cracker, Jean says, "I'm sorry. I must be dense because I don't see how that slogan would appeal to shoppers." (F)

7. When discussing the company's sales bonus program with a close friend, Jerry says, "The prizes are nice, but I want to beat out all the other salespeople to prove I'm the best." (M)

8. In discussing with a colleague the difficulty in deciding which subordinate to pick to work on a very exciting project, Kerry says, "I want you to understand that both people are very capable, and I don't want either to feel slighted by my decision. (F)

9. When sitting on the back porch at a family reunion, Pat was heard saying, "My relationship with John has been under a lot of stress lately because he refuses to discuss our problems. (F)

10. In a conference to discuss an impending lawsuit brought against the company by a dismissed employee, Leslie says, "Who's to blame can be decided later. Right now I want to know what it's going to cost us." (M)

11. At the coffee machine, Kelly can be overheard saying to another worker, "Yeah, I agree. That new software program is awesome, but it follows the same protocols as an earlier version so it will be relatively easy to put into use." (M)

12. When the bookkeeper explains that she's late for the third day in a row because her car broke down again, Logan says, "Don't you think it's time you got a more reliable car?" (F)

# TEAM LEADING ROLES

| | |
|---|---|
| **TOPIC** | Team leading roles |
| | Much of the work of the learning organization is planned during team meetings. At any given time, members may be leading the group in the role of facilitator, trainer, or presenter. If the occasion calls for engaging in group decision making, a member plays the role of facilitator. If the occasion requires the acquisition of new skills, a member may take on the role of trainer. If the team is to receive prepared information in the form of a report, the member providing the information may assume the role of presenter. It is important for team members to be able to know how and when to assume the respective roles. |
| **LEARNING OBJECTIVE** | Participants will be able to appropriately assume the roles of facilitator, trainer, and presenter. |
| **NUMBER OF PARTICIPANTS** | Any number |
| **PLAYING TIME** | 10-12 minutes |
| **REQUIRED MATERIALS** | Pencils, Team Leading Roles Worksheets, flip chart, and markers |

**TO PLAY**

1. Discuss the concept of three team-leading roles.
2. Go over the learning objective for the game.
3. Explain to players they are now going to test their knowledge of three team-leading roles, presenter, trainer, and facilitator.
4. Pass out pencils and copies of Team-Leading Roles Worksheet #1.
5. Go over the directions at the top of the worksheet.
6. Give players two minutes to draw their lines.
7. Give the correct answers, having participants check their own responses.
8. Repeat steps five through seven with Team-Leading Roles Worksheets #2 and #3.
9. Declare players with the most correctly drawn lines winners.
10. Debrief players. On a flip chart, list the three team-leading roles. Under each role list times when it is

most appropriate for the person leading a team to assume that particular role. Have players discuss which of the three roles brings about the most group learning. Ask their opinions on the role they believe to be the most challenging to play and which role they feel most comfortable carrying out. Get players to give reasons for their answers.

**VARIATION**  Play the game according to the above directions but this time use real examples from your own company. The worksheet can also be constructed to have two, as opposed to only one, correct answer (i.e., straight lines). Worksheets could also be constructed using other group roles such as manager, sales person, mediator, or consultant.

**FOR MORE INFORMATION**  Hackett, D. & Martin, C. L. (1993). *Facilitation skills for team leaders*. Menlo Park, CA: Crisp Publishing, Inc.

Answer Trainer Roles: line through bottom row across
Answer Presenter Roles: line down the right-hand column
Answer Facilitator Roles: diagonal line from bottom left to top right

# Team-Leading Roles #1
## (The Trainer Role)

**Directions**: First read each of the nine mini case studies below. Draw a line through three squares, in either a horizontal, vertical, or diagonal row, which contain cases calling for the "trainer" team-leading role.

| | | |
|---|---|---|
| The company must find the best way to comply with customers' demands for quicker response time for emergency repair calls. | Employees are unsure of how the new retirement options may affect them. | Teachers must be made aware of the new district-wide policies regarding student misconduct in the classroom. |
| Management is concerned that even with new safety devices installed on assembly line machinery, many injuries are occurring. | The members of the sales team know very little about the new car models coming out this season. | Management is concerned that employees are not supporting the new customer service policies. |
| New laboratory technicians need to learn their way around the hospital departments. | A newly hired waitress doesn't know how to properly use the computer system to place customer orders. | An office manager sees the difficulty workers have in operating a copy machine. |

# Team-Leading Roles #2
## (The Presenter Role)

**Directions**: First read each of the nine mini case studies below. Draw a line through three squares, in either a horizontal, vertical, or diagonal row, which contain cases calling for the "presenter" team-leading role.

| | | |
|---|---|---|
| A competitor offers a new service to its customers. The feasibility of your company offering a similar type of service is in question. | An office manager sees the difficulty workers have in operating a copy machine. | Employees are unsure of how the new retirement options may affect them. |
| A newly hired waitress doesn't know how to properly use the computer system to place customer orders. | Management is concerned that employees are not supporting the new customer service policies. | Teachers must be made aware of the new district-wide policies regarding student misconduct in the classroom. |
| Management is concerned that even with new safety devices installed on assembly line machinery, many injuries are occurring. | The company must find the best way to comply with customers' demands for quicker response time for emergency repair calls. | The members of the sales team know very little about the new car models coming out this season. |

# Team-Leading Roles #3
## (The Facilitator Role)

**Directions**: First read each of the nine mini case studies below. Draw a line through three squares, in either a horizontal, vertical, or diagonal row, which contain cases calling for the "facilitator" team-leading role.

| | | |
|---|---|---|
| Employees are unsure of how the new retirement options may affect them. | Teachers must be made aware of the new district-wide policies regarding student misconduct in the classroom. | A competitor offers a new service to its customers. The feasibility of your company offering a similar type of service is in question. |
| A newly hired waitress doesn't know how to properly use the computer system to place customer orders. | Management is concerned that employees are not supporting the new customer service policies. | An office manager sees the difficulty workers have in operating a copy machine. |
| Management is concerned that even with new safety devices installed on assembly line machinery, many injuries are occurring. | New laboratory technicians necd to learn their way around the hospital departments. | The members of the sales team know very little about the new car models coming out this season. |

# UNMENTIONABLES

| | |
|---|---|
| **TOPIC** | Open communication |

While seldom acknowledged, most organizations have skeletons, dirty laundry, and/or past snafus they would rather not have discussed. Skeletons might be the weird or antisocial behavior of a key figure in the company. The CEO who regularly takes nips from a bottle of scotch hidden in a desk drawer or a VP who makes sexual advances to women who work for him could be considered skeletons. Examples of dirty laundry are unlawful acts or deceitful practices of a company, such as selling products to a federal agency at elevated prices or not informing consumers of possible hazards of product use. Snafus are business screwups, such as the costly development and introduction of a product that didn't sell or too quickly copying a competitor's new business practice, only to find out that it didn't work for either of them.

The discussion of such topics may be limited to very private conversations among two or three coworkers. In team and other official meetings it may be forbidden to bring to light anything that might negatively reflect on the company or individuals in key management positions. Such practices may inhibit free and open discussion in team meetings. Furthermore, they can prevent employees from learning from the company's past mistakes.

**LEARNING OBJECTIVE**

Participants will be able to engage in more open communication during team meetings.

**NUMBER OF PARTICIPANTS**

Any number

**PLAYING TIME**

15-20 minutes

**REQUIRED MATERIALS**

Pencils, set of Unmentionable Cards, long clothesline, plastic clothespins, flip chart, and markers

**TO PLAY**

1. Stretch a 20-to-30 foot clothesline across the room prior to the game.
2. Introduce players to the topic of unmentionables.

3. Go over the learning objective for the game.
4. Explain to players that they are going to have the opportunity to air some of the types of unmentionables they have personally observed in various workplaces. The person(s) who pins up the most unmentionables in a five-minute time period will be considered the winner(s).
5. Pass a pencil and an Unmentionable Card to each player.
6. Place clothespins and extra Unmentionable Cards near each end of the clothesline.
7. Advise players that when you say "Go" they are to write down on the back of their Unmentionable card an example (of which they have personal knowledge) of a skeleton, dirty laundry, or snafu never publicly acknowledged or discussed. Afterward, they are to pin the Unmentionable Card to the clothesline and pick up a new card on which to write another unmentionable. The process continues for five full minutes. Players must keep track of the number of cards they have pinned to the clothesline
8. Inform players that when you call "Stop," they are to immediately return to their seats and/or lay down their pencils.
9. Call "Go."
10. Five minutes later call "Stop."
11. Identify the player or players who hung up the most Unmentionable Cards.
12. Debrief players. Ask participants to go to the clothesline and retrieve an Unmentionable Card, preferably not one of their own cards. Ask volunteers to read the contents of their cards. After each card is read, discuss how not acknowledging or discussing such a thing can stifle communication and learning within a company. Also discuss how public knowledge of the happening or situation might damage the company or individual careers. On a flip chart, list strategies organizations might use to encourage open communication and learning from mistakes and at the same time not do harm to the organization or to people's careers.

**VARIATION**   Instead of passing out one Unmentionable Card, provide players with three cards. Have them write an example of a skeleton (weird or antisocial behavior on the part of company founders or leaders), dirty laundry (unlawful or deceitful business practice), and snafu (major mistake or mishap) example on the respective cards. Have three separate areas in the room on which to tack the cards. Players writing and tacking up examples of all three types of unmentionables during a three-minute period are considered winners. Follow step 12 above for debriefing purposes.

**FOR MORE INFORMATION**    Senge, P., Roberts, C., Ross, R., Smith, B., & Kleiner, A. (1995). *The fifth discipline fieldbook.* New York: Doubleday.

## Unmentionable Cards

To prepare a set of Unmentionable Cards, photocopy the following and cut out individual items.

# Chapter Seven

# Parts and Engines Games

# Archetyping

TOPIC

Archetype diagrams

Archetypes are cause-and-effect diagrams representing sets of behaviors frequently found in organizations. Arching arrows are used to depict causal relationships among various elements of a system (i.e., organization). To show the cyclical nature of most relationships, archetype diagrams take on a circular shape, complete with feedback loops. The feedback loops represent how elements act as both causes and effects in relationship to other elements in the system.

The five common archetypes found in organizations iare called "backfire," "growth stunter," "symptoms treating," "dried-up oasis," and "unexpected opponents." *Backfires* are quick fixes that alleviate the problem temporarily but in the long run aggravate the problem. An example of a backfire would be borrowing money on one credit card to make a payment on another.

*Growth stunters* occur when a company focuses on growth, but spends no time on developing plans for coping with a potential slowdown in business. An example of a growth stunter might be a chief executive enjoying support for downsizing her or his company, but not having a plan to deal with waning support when cuts in popular programs are needed to achieve the desired result.

*Symptoms treating* refers to addressing a side effect rather than the real source of a problem. For instance, every time a certain production line falls behind, management pulls workers from other areas in to help the line catch up, but doesn't deal with the problem that causes the line to fall behind in the first place.

A *dried-up oasis* happens when two or more groups or organizations work together to develop a common resource, which ends up with so many demands made on it that it becomes impossible for the respective parties to have their needs met. An example of a dried-up oasis might be for two similar companies to develop a joint product repair service to make use of limited local repair technicians, only to give the technicians so much work that they can't keep up with the demands.

*Unexpected opponents* are two groups or organizations that work together to meet the needs of each other, but find themselves at odds when it comes to the methods by which their respective goals will be achieved. For example, to boost sales, a manufacturer and a grocery store chain join on a promotion for canned vegetables. The manufacturer supplies the canned goods at a sharply reduced price. The grocery chain buys large quantities and still has a huge stock of the vegetables after the sale to sell at regular price. The grocery chain makes extra profits while the disgruntled manufacturer loses because the chain does not need to reorder at regular prices for some time.

To use archetypes in gaining a better understanding of an organization problem, team members must first hypothesize what might be creating a problem or issue in the company. The next step is to select an archetype which most closely matches the hypothesized organization behavior. Finally, the team tests the archetype in terms of their organization, much like they might test the applicability of any mental model.

**LEARNING OBJECTIVE**

Participants will be able to recognize reoccurring behavior patterns commonly found in their organizations.

**NUMBER OF PARTICIPANTS**

Any number

**PLAYING TIME**

20-30 minutes

**REQUIRED MATERIALS**

Pencils markers, large sheets of paper, and copies of the Archetyping Puzzle

**TO PLAY**

1. Introduce participants to the concept of archetypes.
2. Go over the learning objective for the game.
3. Inform players that they are about to play a simple puzzle game that tests their knowledge of five archetypes.
4. Pass out a pencil and a copy of the Archetyping Puzzle to each player.
5. Go over the directions to the game.
6. Tell players to begin.
7. After three minutes call "Stop."
8. Give the correct answers to the puzzle, with players checking their own work for accuracy.

9. Declare players who correctly identified all four diagrams winners.
10. Debrief players. Divide players into five groups and assign each group a different archetype. Provide each group with a marker and a large sheet of paper. Ask each group to think of a time and organization in which their assigned archetype may have been operating. Have them give the company a fictitious name and draw an archetype diagram depicting the archetype behavior operating in the company. Request that the groups share their archetype examples with one another.

**VARIATION**

Provide each participant a small piece of paper containing the name of an archetype, a large blank sheet of paper, and a marker. Give players five minutes to draw an archetype diagram depicting the behavior category written on their small piece of paper. After five minutes, have players go around the room and have other players guess the behavior their archetype diagram depicts. The first person to get three people to correctly identify the archetype becomes the winner of the game.

**FOR MORE INFORMATION**

Senge, P., Roberts, C., Ross, R., Smith, B. & Kleiner, A. (1994). *The fifth discipline fieldbook*. New York: Doubleday.

Answers: Top left -- symptoms treating; Top right -- Backfire; Bottom left -- Growth stunter; Bottom right -- Unexpected opponents

# Archetyping Puzzle

**Directions**: Carefully examine each of the archetype diagrams below. Under each diagram write its type. The diagrams may be one of the following types: <u>Backfire</u>, <u>Dried-Up Oasis</u>, <u>Growth Stunter</u>, <u>Symptoms Treating</u>, or <u>Unexpected Opponents</u>.

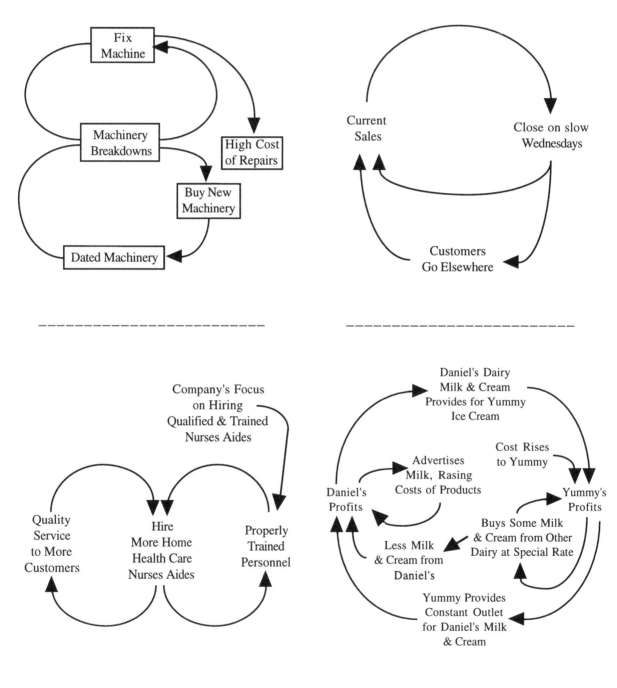

# FISHBONE PUZZLE

TOPIC

Cause-and-effect diagram

As employees attempt to better understand issues and challenges within their organization, they are faced with sorting out how various events and conditions are related to one another. One such relationship is whether an event or condition is operating as a cause or an effect. In many instances an event or condition can operate as both cause and effect.

A commonly used visual tool to help groups analyze and discuss cause-and-effect relationships is the fishbone diagram. As its name implies, the diagram takes the form of a fish skeleton. An organization issue or challenge is printed at the head portion of the fishbone. This serves as the "effect" for further analysis and discussion. Pointing to the fishhead (i.e., effect) is a long arrow. It represents the fish's spine. Attached to the spine are lines representing the larger bones of the fish. These bones are treated as potential causes. They are given fairly broad labels. Connected to each large bone are smaller bones. These branches of smaller bones depict subcauses related to the broader categories.

LEARNING
OBJECTIVE

Participants will be able to use a fishbone diagram to explore cause-and-effect relationships in their organizations.

NUMBER OF
PARTICIPANTS

Any number

PLAYING TIME

15-20 minutes

REQUIRED
MATERIALS

Pencils, Fishbone Diagram, flip chart, and markers

TO PLAY

1. Introduce players to the concept of fishbone diagrams.
2. Go over the learning objective for the game.
3. Inform players that they will be divided into groups and provided with a fishbone diagram to complete. The first group to complete the diagram will be asked to share their answers with the audience. All

groups who complete the puzzle within five minutes will be considered winners.

4. Divide participants into groups of four to five players.
5. Pass out pencils and copies of the Fishbone Diagram.
6. Go over the directions to the puzzle.
7. Give participants five minutes to complete the puzzle.
8. After five minutes, declare all groups who have completed the puzzle winners and "tellers of the best fish stories."
9. Debrief players. Ask a member of the group that finished first to come forward and draw the group's fish bone diagram on a flip chart, one large bone at a time. As each set of smaller branches is filled, discuss the specific causes with the audience. Invite participants to agree or disagree with the specific causes. Ask for examples of other potential causes. On the flip chart, list how a fishbone diagram might be used to analyze other types of relationships in an organization.

**VARIATION**

Discuss various organization issues of concern to participants. Prioritize the issues and select one of the top priorities for the purpose of constructing a fishbone diagram. Divide players into small groups to brainstorm the general cause categories to be used in the fishbone puzzle. After three minutes, reconvene as a large group to select the five broad cause categories to be placed on the puzzle. Pass out pencils and copies of blank fishbone diagrams to participants. Have them fill in the issue (effect) in the head section and the names of the large bones (cause categories). Play the game according to the above directions (i.e., steps six through nine).

**FOR MORE INFORMATION**

Hackett, D. & Martin, C. L. (1993). *Facilitation skills for team leaders.* Menlo Park, CA: Crisp Publications, Inc.

### Fishbone Diagram Directions

Pretend that you have been asked by the management of Citizen's Mutual Insurance Company to brainstorm some of the potential causes of its unusually high employee turnover rate. Citizen's Mutual is a medium-sized nationwide organization. It has been in business for over 75 years, with its corporate headquarters in Chicago. For the past five years, Citizen's employee turnover rate has steadily increased. In the past two years, the turnover rate has been twice the national average for insurance companies of comparable size. With the cost of replacing employees also steadily increasing, high employee turnover is an expensive problem.

Beside each small line on the Fishbone Diagram write in a potential turnover cause. Each cause must related to the causal subgroups to which the small lines are attached. For example, the causes branching off from the equipment bone must relate to causes related to equipment resources. You have five minutes to write in 16 potential causes of high employee turnover at Citizen's Mutual Insurance Company.

# Fishbone Diagram

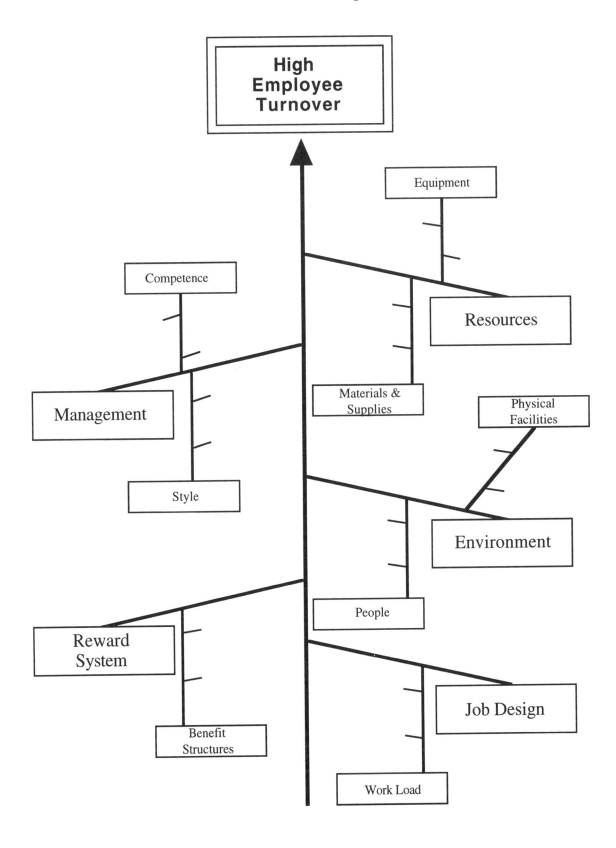

# Fishbone Diagram
(blank)

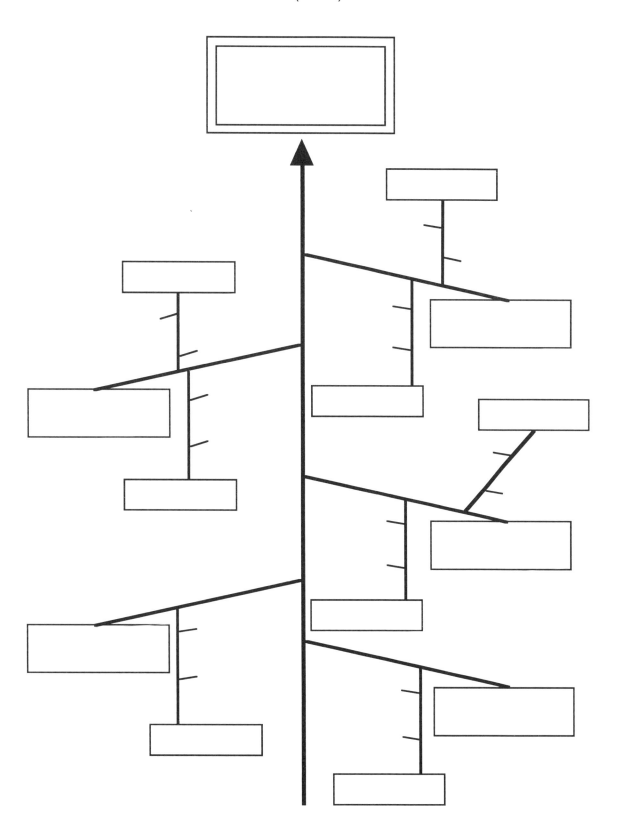

# HUMAN FLOW CHART

TOPIC

Flow charting

Flow charts are graphic representations of various steps or procedures involved in a process. The chart typically depicts a set of sequential events leading to an outcome. Flow charts can help employees understand the actual or desired flow of information, paper, raw materials, and/or finished products. Flow charting makes use of such symbols as double rectangles (critical steps), ovals (beginnings and endings), arrows (movement and direction), rectangles (activities not involving a decision), diamonds (alternative decisions), and exaggerated capital "D"s (delays or holds).

LEARNING
OBJECTIVE

Participants will be able to construct a flow chart that represents an important process in their organization.

NUMBER OF
PARTICIPANTS

Any number in groups of 10

PLAYING TIME

12-15 minutes

REQUIRED
MATERIALS

A set of Human Flow Chart kit for each ten players, straight pins, flip chart, and markers

TO PLAY

1. Introduce participants to the concept of flow charting and commonly used charting symbols.
2. Go over the learning objective for the game.
3. Inform players that they will be given a flow chart symbol, an arrow, and two straight pins. The symbol is but one piece needed to a complete flow chart.
4. Explain that upon receiving the symbol, they are to pin the piece to their blouses or shirts. They will then be given three minutes to join with others in the room to form a human flow chart that graphically depicts the preparation of a holiday gelatin mold. Any group correctly forming the human flow chart will be considered winners.
5. With the exception of the players receiving the end symbol, provide each player with a symbol, an arrow, and two straight pins. The player with an end symbol does not need an arrow. Ask that they

pin the symbol to their blouses or shirts. Arrows are pinned to the left of the symbols.

6. Tell players to begin forming flow charts.
7. As soon as a correct flow chart is formed, check it for accuracy. If correct, declare members of the chart winners. If a correct chart is not formed within three minutes, call "Stop." Ask players to return to their original positions.
8. Repeat steps six and seven until a group successfully constructs the flow chart.
9. Debrief players. Ask players to list processes within their organizations which could be graphically depicted with a flow chart. Discuss how the construction of such flow charts might help workers understand the work of the organization. List on a flip chart, ways the interrelatedness of organization elements or parts might be graphically depicted other than with flow charts.

**VARIATION**

Divide participants into teams of 10 members each and supply them with three copies of the Human Flow Chart symbols, straight pins, and black markers. Give groups 10 minutes to form a human flow chart that represents a process that would be familiar to everyone in the audience. At the end of 10 minutes have each group come forward and form a human flow chart. Declare all groups winners who correctly use the symbols to represent a real process with which other players are familiar.

**FOR MORE INFORMATION**

Hackett, D. & Martin, C. L. (1993). *Facilitation skills for team leaders*. Menlo Park, CA: Crisp Publications, Inc.

Answers:

1. Start, 2. Pour 2 small boxes of gelatin into bowl, 3. Stir in 2 cups boiling water, 4. Stir in 2 cups cold water, 5. Refrigerate until gelatin starts to thicken, 6. Stir in 2 cups fruit, 7. Pour into mold, 8. Chill until firm, 9. Unmold gelatin onto plate, 10. End.

## Human Flow Chart Kit

To prepare materials for one Flow Chart Kit, photocopy the following items and cut out individual pieces.

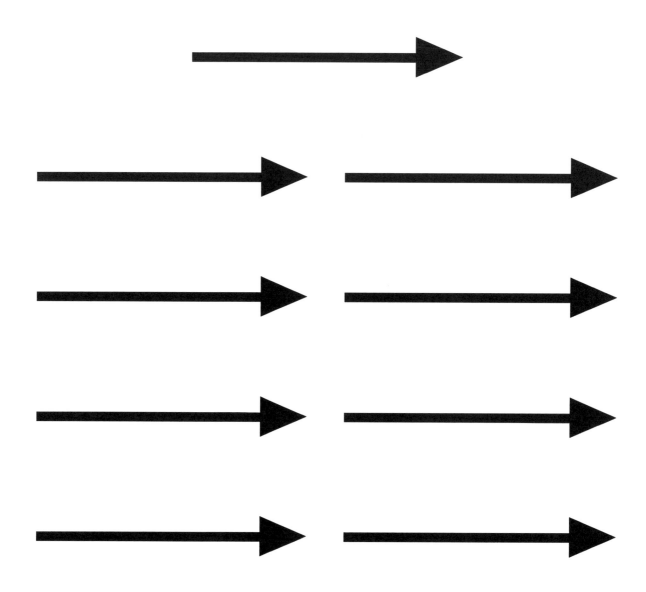

Unmold
gelatin
onto
plate.

Stir in 2 cups
boiling water
to dissolve
gelatin.

Stir in
2 cups
cold
water.

Pour
into
8 cup
mold.

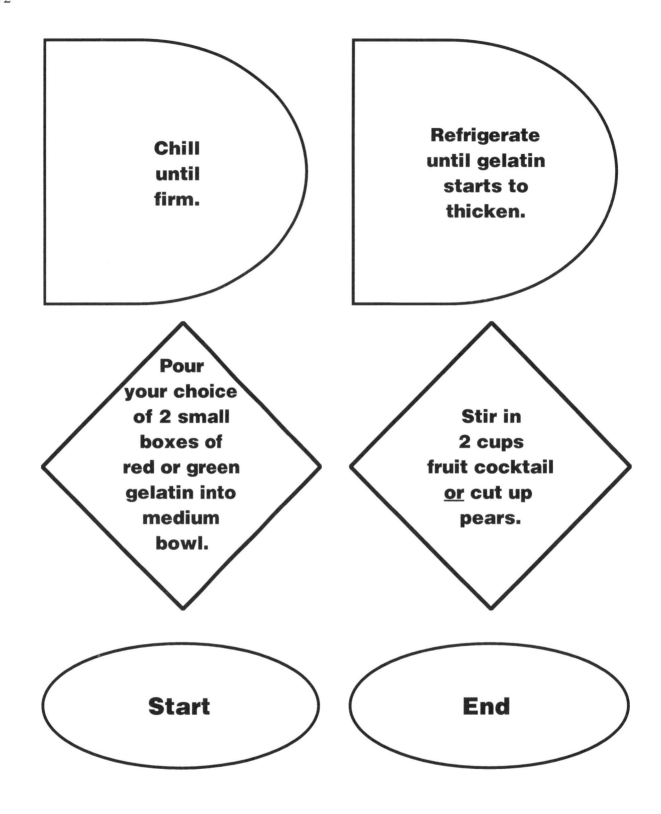

Chill until firm.

Refrigerate until gelatin starts to thicken.

Pour your choice of 2 small boxes of red or green gelatin into medium bowl.

Stir in 2 cups fruit cocktail **or** cut up pears.

Start

End

## Blank Human Flow Chart Kit

To prepare materials for a custom-made Flow Chart Kit, type desired steps or elements on the following blank symbols. Photocopy items and cut out individual pieces.

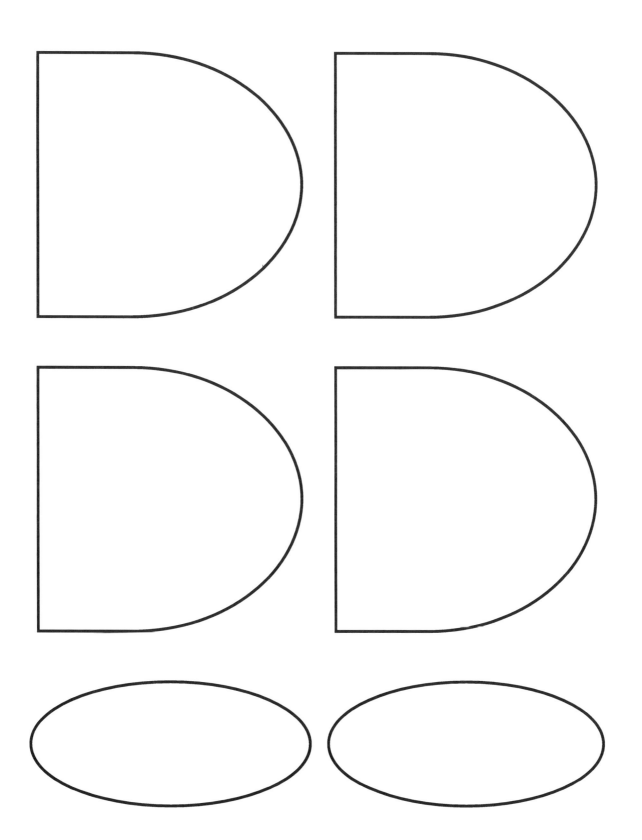

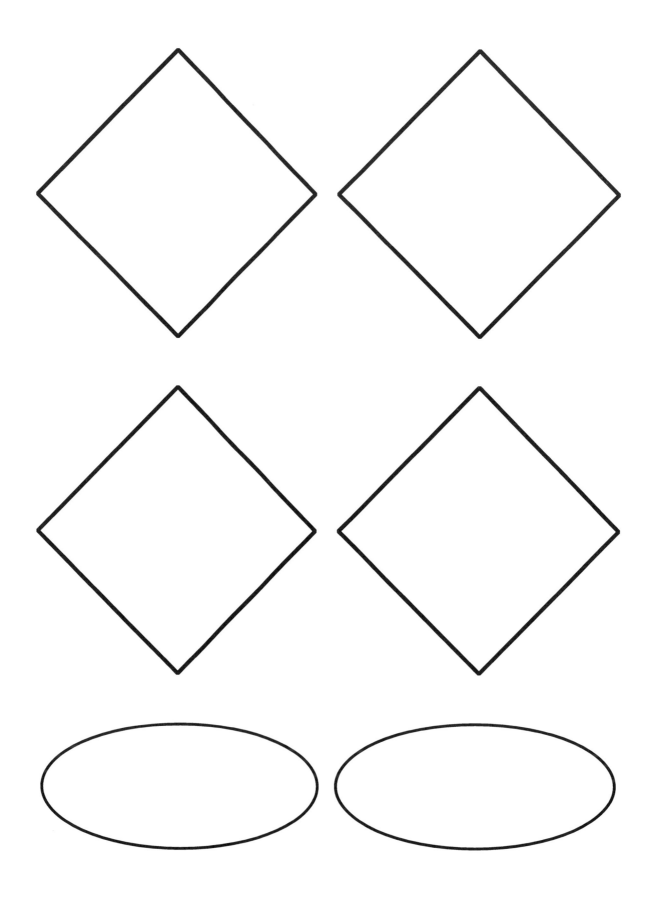

# LIFE CYCLE

**TOPIC**  Company life cycles

Many organization experts agree that companies pass through predictable developmental stages and/or economic cycles. As is the case with humans, companies have a beginning (i.e., a birth), experience growth, become mature, and eventually cease to exist (i.e., die). The life stage a company is in, as well as current economic conditions, foretell the challenges an organization is likely to be facing. A better understanding of the life cycle of organizations and the predictable challenges they are apt to face can help employees plan and rehearse for such events.

**LEARNING OBJECTIVE**  Participants will be able to associate various developmental tasks with stages in an organization's life cycle.

**NUMBER OF PARTICIPANTS**  Any number divided into groups of four players

**PLAYING TIME**  20-25 minutes

**REQUIRED MATERIALS**  One die, paper clips of different colors, a deck of Life Cycle Question Cards, and a Life Cycle Game board for every four players

**TO PLAY**

1. Introduce players to the concept of organization life cycles.
2. Go over the learning objective for the game.
3. Inform participants that they are about to play a simple board game called the Life Cycle. The object of the game is to be the first person in the group to get completely around the game board.
4. Explain that on correctly answering a question on one of the Life Cycle Question Cards, players will roll a die to determine the number of spaces they advance that turn.
5. Divide participants into groups of four players.
6. Provide each group a die, four paper clips of different colors, a deck of Life Cycle Question Cards, and The Life Cycle Game board. All game materials should be placed in the center of each group.

7. Ask a person in each group to shuffle the deck of Life Cycle Question Cards and place the cards facedown in the middle of the game board.

8. Direct players to select different color paper clips as markers and to place their markers on the Start-Up space of their respective boards.

9. Instruct players to roll the die once to determine who plays first. The person rolling the highest number goes first.

10. Tell participants that the person to the immediate left of the first player is to now pick the top Life Cycle Question Card from the deck and read the question to the first player. If the player answers the question correctly, she or he is to roll the die and advance around the board in a clockwise direction that number of spaces. If she or he does not answer the question correctly, her or his marker remains in its current space and play continues in a clockwise direction around the group.

11. Advise players that question cards must be returned to the bottom of the deck after each person's turn.

12. Explain that if a player lands on one of three setback spaces (i.e., fire, lawsuit, loss of major client) she or he must move back the designated spaces.

13. Ask players to continue playing in a clockwise direction around the group until a player reaches the Personnel Changes space on the board. That player is the winner for that group. Players do not have to roll the exact number of spaces to land on the Personnel Changes space. They need only roll a high enough number to reach it.

14. Debrief players. Have participants identify the stage (i.e., start-up, early growth, later growth, stable) through which their employing organization is currently cycling. Ask for the reasons they believe their organization is in the stated life cycle stage. Discuss whether they believe the challenges faced by the organization in this particular stage are mainly external or internal.

**VARIATION**

Construct a set of Life Cycle Question Cards based on the history (life cycles) of your own company and play the game according to the above directions.

**FOR MORE INFORMATION**

Churchill, N.C. & Lewis, V. L. (1983, May, June). The five stages of small business growth. *Harvard Business Review*, pp. 30-50.

Dodge, H. R. & Robbins, J. E. (1992, January). An empirical investigation of the organizational life cycle model for small business development survival. *Journal of Small Business Management*, 30, 27-27.

Mintzberg, H. (1984). Power and organization life cycles. *Academy of Management Review*, 9, 207-224.

## Life Cycle Question Cards

To prepare one deck of Life Cycle Question Cards, photocopy the following items on card-stock paper and cut them out.

True or false, management priorities change during each life cycle. (T)

True or false, in the early stages of development businesses are more preoccupied with external challenges than with internal challenges. (T)

True or false, being able to expand from one basic customer, product, or service to a broader base should be a key consideration when starting a business. (T)

True or false, an organizational structure or organizational plan is usually not well developed in the start-up stage. (T)

True or false, power in the start-up stage of a business is usually exclusively in the hands of the owner(s). (T)

True or false, filling a void left by other companies may be a valid purpose for starting a new business. (T)

True or false, location is only important because of the costs involved in a start-up stage. (F, also of major importance in the location decision is closeness to customers and/or supplies or raw materials.)

True or false, customer contact is a major problem in the start-up stage of a business. (T)

True or false, the early growth stage might also be seen as the survival stage because the business may just be breaking even. (T)

True or false, in the early growth stage a manager usually takes on half the power of the owner. (F, the owner retains most if not all control of decision making and direction for the business.)

True or false, the accounting system is usually set up in the early growth stage. (T)

True or false, during the early growth stage conflict with owner decisions and ideals is a serious problem. (F, the owners vision and direction is not questioned.)

True or false, the early growth stage may be characterized by the attempt to increase markets for the products or services of the business. (T)

True or false, businesses usually try to gain control of outside forces affecting them in the early growth stage. (F, they usually react to the external environment rather than attempt to exert any control over it.)

True or false, businesses in early growth may struggle with controlling costs while increasing the production of products or services to meet increased demand. (T)

True or false, lack of business knowledge may be a serious problem in the formation stage. (T)

True or false, sales will grow at an increased rate during the later growth period. (F, at this point sales growth slows or levels off.)

True or false, a decision to expand or maintain the status quo is a major consideration during the later growth stage. (T)

True or false, advertising may need to be stepped up in order to offset increased competition in the later growth stage. (T)

True or false, assessing market conditions and identifying new markets is only necessary in the later stages of growth. (F, it is important in all stages of the life cycle.)

True or false, delegation of responsibility by the founder increases during the later growth stage. (T)

True or false, over time, it is possible for a business to prosper without growing larger or expanding its products or services. (T)

284

True or false, as a business matures, smaller subunits may experience increased conflict or political maneuvering. (T)

True or false, cleaning out inefficiencies becomes important once a business becomes stable. (T)

True or false, a need for, but resistance to, change is characteristic of the mature company. (T)

True or false, a business can usually remain under the command of the owner during the mature stage with little or no detriment to the growth of the business. (F, though the owner may retain the major financial interest, fresh ideas are usually necessary to promote growth when owner creativity and enthusiasm may be waning.)

True or false, if a company in the start-up stage can deliver the product, getting customers will not be a problem. (F, the company must not only be able to deliver the product, but also ensure that there are customers who want it.)

True or false, the biggest factor in survival of a business is having a large amount of money on hand at start-up time. (F, sufficient finances are one consideration, but not the largest. A good product or service, customers, and advertising are also very important.)

True or false, usually in the stable stage of a business's development, markets are firmly established and advertising becomes less important. (F, competition increases and to retain sales or experience further sales growth, advertising is extremely important.)

True or false, both large and small businesses go through the same life cycle stages. (T)

True or false, in the mature stage of development, a business may choose to relocate or expand some or all of its activities. (T)

True or false, in order to remain in existence in the mature stage, a company may need to change its product or service line or diversify. (T)

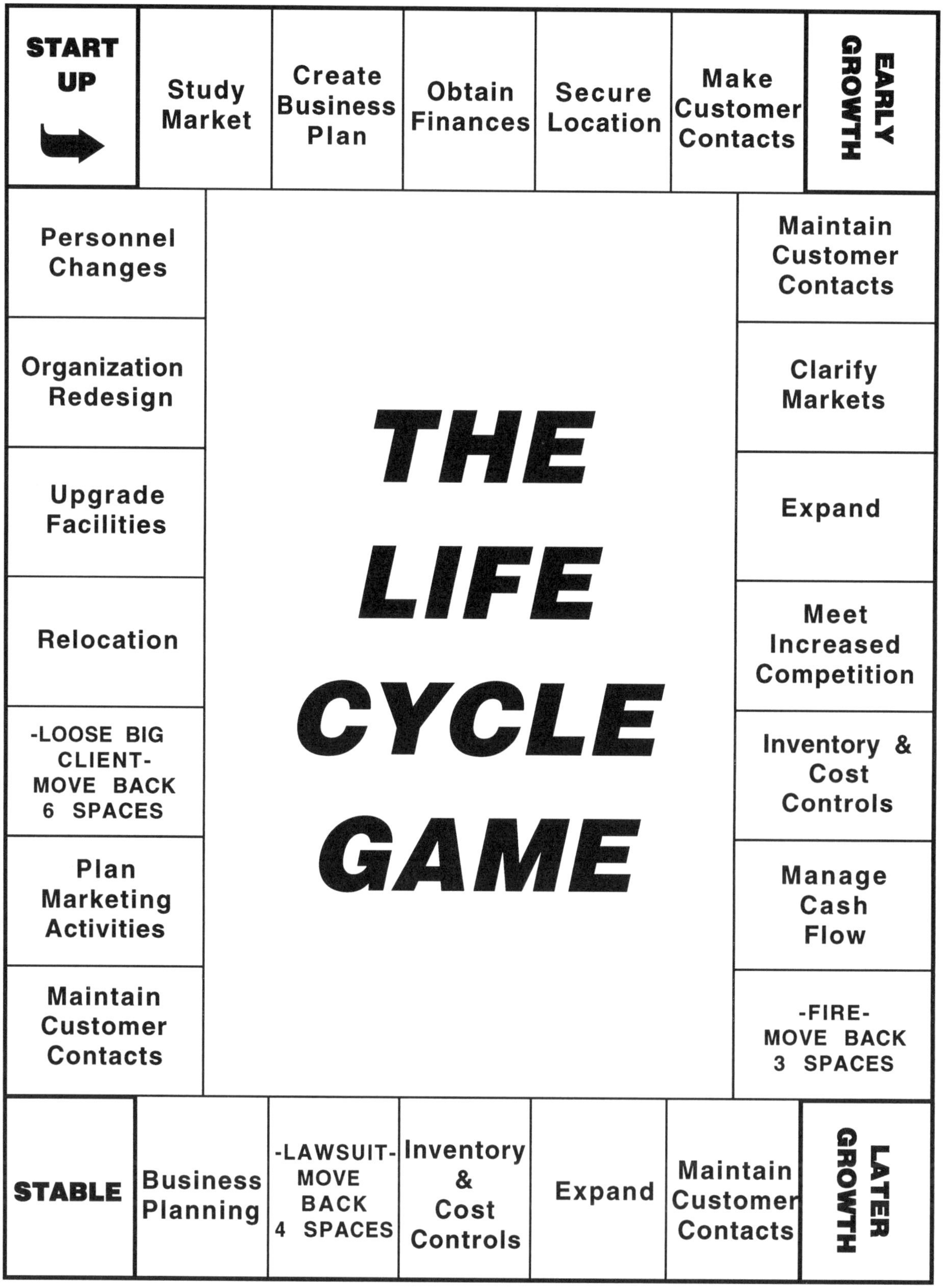
START UP
Study Market
Create Business Plan
Obtain Finances
Secure Location
Make Customer Contacts
EARLY GROWTH
Maintain Customer Contacts
Clarify Markets
Expand
Meet Increased Competition
Inventory & Cost Controls
Manage Cash Flow
-FIRE- MOVE BACK 3 SPACES
LATER GROWTH
Maintain Customer Contacts
Expand
Inventory & Cost Controls
-LAWSUIT- MOVE BACK 4 SPACES
Business Planning
STABLE
Maintain Customer Contacts
Plan Marketing Activities
-LOOSE BIG CLIENT- MOVE BACK 6 SPACES
Relocation
Upgrade Facilities
Organization Redesign
Personnel Changes
THE LIFE CYCLE GAME

# MIND OR SOUL

| | |
|---|---|
| **TOPIC** | Structural and human subsystems |

In the 1960s Robert Blake and Jane Mouton introduced their famous "Managerial Grid." Their two-dimensional nine-point scale highlighted the existence of two major subsystems within organizations--the structural and the human. The structural (referred to by Blake and Mouton as "production") system pertains to such matters as raw materials, manufacturing and/or service delivery processes, and organization structure. The human or people subsystem has to do with employee morale and motivation, interpersonal relations, and work skills. To be a viable organization, companies must learn how to make improvements in both systems. To neglect one at the expense of the other is to place the organization at risk.

**LEARNING OBJECTIVE**

Participants will be able to identify when an organization needs to focus more on structural concerns and when it needs to pay greater attention to people matters.

**NUMBER OF PARTICIPANTS**

Any number

**PLAYING TIME**

10-15 minutes

**REQUIRED MATERIALS**

One Soul and one Mind playing card for each player, a set of Soul/Mind Scenarios printed on small pieces of paper, pencils, flip chart, and markers

**TO PLAY**

1. Introduce players to the concept of two organization subsystems, structural and human.
2. Go over the learning objective for the game.
3. Tell players that they are going to be read 12 short scenarios. They will have to decide whether the events call for paying greater attention to the human (soul) or the technical (mind) aspects of the situation at hand.
4. Pass out two playing cards to each player (i.e., one Soul and one Mind card). Ask players to place their cards facedown in front of them.
5. Explain that after each scenario has been read, they are to turn up either their Soul or their Mind

card. If they believe the situation demands greater attention be given to the human side of the case, they should place their Soul card faceup. If, on the other hand, they believe the situation demands greater attention be given to technical or structural matters, they should place their Mind card faceup.

6. Advise players that anyone getting at least 12 of the 14 scenarios correct, becomes a first-place winner. Players who get at least 10 of the 14 cases become second-place winners.

7. Pass out slips of paper containing the scenarios to 14 participants (if there are less than 14 players, some individuals may receive more than one scenario.)

8. One at a time, ask participants to read their scenarios aloud.

9. Direct players to place either their Mind or Soul card faceup.

10. After each scenario, give the correct answer and ask players to keep track of any incorrect answers they accumulate.

11. After all of the scenarios have been read, determine which players have missed no more than two. Declare them first-place winners. Next determine who missed no more than four answers, declare them second-place winners.

12. Debrief players. Ask participants which subsystem receives more attention at their organizations-- people matters or structural and task matters. Have players speculate on why this is the case. Solicit brief examples (real incidents) from the audience telling about a company that focused on people when it should have paid attention to structure. Solicit brief examples of a company that focused on structure when it should have paid more attention to people. On a flip chart, list ways managers and/or work teams can learn to focus on both the human and the structural systems in their organizations at the same time.

**VARIATION**

Pass out a lined three-by-five inch index card and pencil to each player. Have players whose last name begins with letters A through J write down a recent challenge faced by their company on the top line of their cards. Have the others write down an aniticpated challenge their company will face in the next three years. Now have players write a short explanation of the challenge they have selected. Ask that they not give the names of any actual companies. Play the game according to Steps 8-11 above.

**FOR MORE**
**INFORMATION** Blake, R., and Mouton, J. (1968). *Building a dynamic corporation through grid organization development.* Reading, MA: Addison-Wesley.

Answers: Soul: 1, 4, 5, 6, 7, 12, 14, Mind: 2, 3, 8, 9, 10, 11, 1 3.

**Playing  Cards**

To prepare a deck of playing cards, photocopy the following items on card-stock paper and cut them out.

| | |
|:---:|:---:|
| *SOUL* | **MIND** |
| *SOUL* | **MIND** |
| *SOUL* | **MIND** |

# Soul/Mind Case Scenarios

1. John has just joined the company. He is very good at his job and catches on to technical matters very quickly. He seems to be at somewhat of a loss in dealing with company policies and politics. In short, he knows how to do his job, but a lot less about how the organization demands the job be done.

2. The office of the Wilson-Beeman Electric Supply Company is a pleasant bustling place. In the six months the firm has been in business, the client roster has tripled. The employees are all proud of the progress of the company, but feel that it still lacks a set of rules for employees. Such things as dress, code of conduct, and guidelines for customer relations are not clearly established.

3. Sam Jones is the office manager for the Magic Money Accounting Agency. New IRS regulations have just been put into effect. He attended a workshop to learn about the new regulations and has a good grasp on how they affect taxpayers. Several of the accountants under him are confused about certain rules even after studying them in their reference guides. Since calling the IRS for clarification takes time away from their work, Sam is likely to be needed as a source of assistance.

4. Several younger investigators at the large Snoopers Inc. detective agency appear bored with their jobs. All are creative, quick learners who seem to thrive on challenging, unusual cases. These people are the type rival agencies are always trying to steal away.

5. The assembly crew of the Restful Sleep Casket Company had been performing at top levels with very little waste and no injuries for over a month. However, in the last week, workers have slowed down and seem tired out. The crew seems to need a shot in the arm to get them going again.

6. Charlie Mitchell's team has routinely outsold the sales team of their rival company. However, they are becoming complacent, and the rival team is catching up. Charlie has complete faith in his team, and he firmly believes that they can rise to the challenge and sell much more, greatly widening the gap between them and their competitors.

7. Microcosm Software, Inc., has dramatically increased its sales of computer software over the past three years. Most of the increase has been due to outstanding word processing and desktop publishing programs. The teams working on the development of games and educational programs feel a bit neglected and not part of the company's growth. Even though their work is very important to the continued success of the company, these workers do not see their role in the organization's future.

8. The Chez Ritzi is an elite restaurant in the high-rent district of the city. Its reputation is built on its exclusiveness, fine quality cuisine, and personalized service. The two new waiters who are starting today have excellent waiting skills and very pleasant personalities. However, both lack work experience in upper-class establishments, such as the Chez. As the manager, Jacques Cardeau, observes the new employees, he sees that they do not do some of the little niceties that the Chez's pampered guests have come to expect. This lack in the waiters' training could offend some of the restaurant's haughty patrons.

9. The homicide division of a large metropolitan police department has a particularly complex murder to solve. The crime involves several suspects, many confused witnesses, but few obvious clues, requiring that a highly trained team of detectives and other personnel be used in the investigation. So that no information is lost, time is of the essence. Tasks will have to be appropriately assigned and coordinated to arrive at an accurate solution efficiently, but the team members are confused about where to start.

10. Everlasting Electronics Company has three large orders which need to be shipped out in the next two weeks. Each order has to be sent out by a different date and each is for a different type of product. Parts of each order will have to be made because there are not enough of the required items in stock. A schedule needs to be quickly drawn up to ensure that enough items are produced and ready to go by the designated shipping date.

11. Employees in the design department of Just Toys have come up with a new action figure series that they feel will take the 5- to 10-year-old age group by storm. It is completely different from anything they or any other toy designers have created before. They need just a few extra days to work out all the fine details of the characters. Then they will need a lot of support in getting the approval of company executives, who have not been very responsive to radical ideas in the past.

12. Barry Burnbridge has been working for Centerville Savings Bank for six months. He graduated from the local university with honors and does most of the technical functions of the job with great accuracy and efficiency. However, at times, it takes Barry twice as long as normally necessary to get the work done. In dealing with a small error or an unfamiliar situation, he gets "tangled up in his own underwear." With help in learning to control these situations, Barry could be an outstanding employee worthy of promotion.

13. The maids are at war with the maintenance people at the Old City Hotel. The maids claim that the maintenance people are slow, at best, in making repairs, sometimes not doing them at all. The maintenance people say that the maids are not explicit in reporting each problem and sometimes forget to report one for several days. No one will take

responsibility in what may be a communication breakdown or the inefficiency of the maids and/or the maintenance people. Meanwhile, hotel patrons are subjected to malfunctioning or broken equipment and fixtures in their rooms.

14. As manager of Harper's Bargain Emporium, Donna Morris has her people skills tested on a daily basis. Already this morning, Bessie Lewis, a clerk in ladies fashions came in late and upset from an accident on the way to work. Then Donna was called to sporting goods to deal with a customer who requested to see the manager about a refund on a damaged exercise bike. She said it didn't work because she didn't lose any weight, so she kicked it and broke her foot. Auggie Barnes in appliances is in a bad mood because his wife left him again. Lila Woods is happy and excited about her new grandchild and looks to Donna for a few kind words. On top of all of this, Donna will shortly have to deal with three visiting company executives. One is a "brisk, no-nonsense grouch," one a "nervous little mouse," and one a "silly old playboy."

# SIX-BOX PUZZLE

| | |
|---|---|
| **TOPIC** | Weisbord's Six-Box Organization Analysis Model |

Weisbord's model consists of six boxes containing different aspects (elements) of an organization (system). The boxes can be used to assess a company's development. They can also be used to diagnose problems existing in an organization. These six organization elements include: (1) purpose, what business the company is in; (2) structure, how work is divided up; (3) relationships, how people work together and manage conflict; (4) rewards, incentives for performing all needed tasks; (5) helpful mechanisms, adequate technologies; and (6) leadership, keeping things in balance. It is important to keep in mind that problems or shortcomings in one area of the organization can adversely affect other elements.

**LEARNING OBJECTIVE**

Participants will be able to analyze an organization using Weisbord's Six-Box Organization Analysis Model.

**NUMBER OF PARTICIPANTS**

Any number

**PLAYING TIME**

7-12 minutes

**REQUIRED MATERIALS**

A copy of the Six-Box Puzzle for every six players, flip chart, and markers

**TO PLAY**

1. Introduce Weisbord's Six-Box Organization Analysis Model.
2. Go over the learning objective for the game.
3. Explain to players that they are going to be given one piece of a six-piece puzzle containing the six areas of analysis of the Weisbord model.
4. Advise players that when you give the signal to begin they are to find five others in the room who have the remaining pieces. The first group to correctly assemble the complete puzzle are to call out "Weisbord." That group is the winner of the game.
5. Pass out a puzzle piece to each participant.
6. Tell players to begin.
7. As soon as a group correctly assembles a puzzle and calls "Weisbord," declare them winners.

8. Debrief players. Divide participants into six groups according to Weisbord's six boxes (i.e., elements). Give each group two minutes to come up with five commonly occurring organization problems within their assigned area. Taking one box at a time, list on a flip chart three examples each group generated. Discuss how some of the problems might spill over into other boxes.

**VARIATIONS**   To make the game slightly more challenging, the facilitator may pass out blank puzzle pieces in place of printed "Rewards" and "Leadership" pieces. Explain to players that they must correctly label all blank pieces when putting their puzzle together.

**FOR MORE INFORMATION**   Weisbord, M. (1976). Organizational designs: Six places to look for trouble with or without a theory. *Group and Organization Studies*, 1, 430-447.

## Six-Box Puzzle

To prepare one Six-Box Puzzle, photocopy the following item on card-stock paper and cut out individual puzzle pieces.

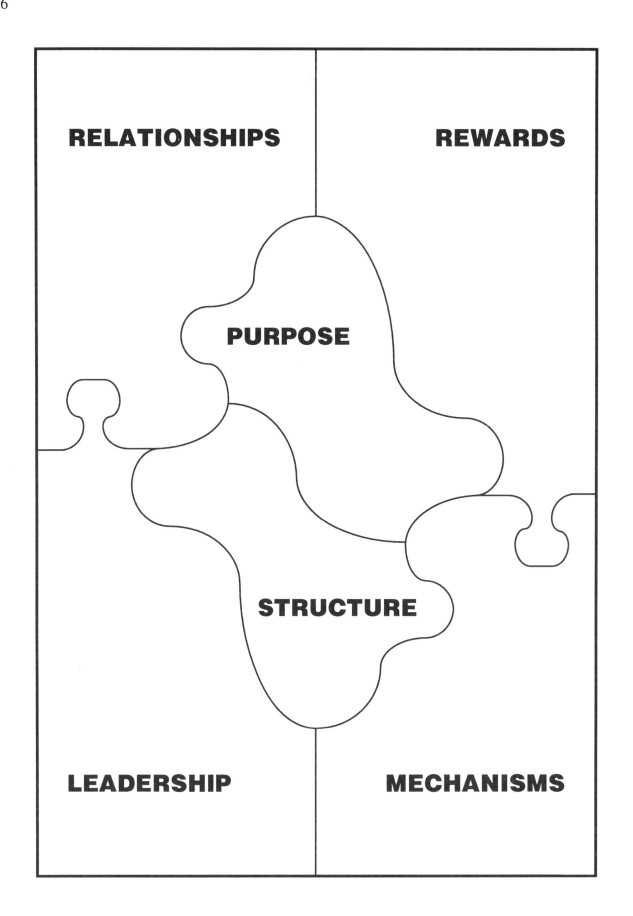

# STORMING NORMING

| | |
|---|---|
| **TOPIC** | Developmental stages of teams |
| | John Orsburn and his associates have identified developmental stages through which they believe most self-directing work teams pass. The stages are often referred to as "forming," "storming," "norming," and "performing." In the forming stage, individuals greatly anticipate team membership and attempt to "feel out" other members. During the storming stage, members are often confused, in conflict, and frustrated. In the norming stage, members commence to come together, start functioning as a team, and begin performing. As a team moves into the performing stage, it functions as a team, solves complex problems, and performs at a very high level. |
| **LEARNING OBJECTIVE** | Participants will be able to identify team member behaviors that typically occur during different stages of a team's development. |
| **NUMBER OF PARTICIPANTS** | Any number |
| **PLAYING TIME** | 7-12 minutes |
| **REQUIRED MATERIALS** | Pencils, copies of the Team Stages Puzzle, flip chart, and markers |

**TO PLAY**

1. Introduce participants to Orsburn's team development stages model.
2. Go over the learning objective for the game.
3. Tell players that they are going to be given a cross-out puzzle which contains the four team development stages: forming, storming, norming, and performing.
4. Pass out pencils and copies of the Team Stages Puzzle to each player. Ask participants not to begin the puzzle until you call "Begin."
5. Go over the directions at the top of the Team Stages Puzzle.
6. Tell players to begin.
7. After five minutes call "Stop."
8. Give the correct answers to the puzzle while players check their responses.

9. Declare individuals who correctly crossed out all items winners.
10. Debrief players. List the four team development stages on a flip chart and ask players to identify other behaviors that might be characteristic of each of the stages. Discuss what might be the appropriate role of the team leader or facilitator during each of the stages. Come up with ideas for preparing team members for the problems that frequently occur in the "storming" stage. Ask participants to come up with strategies teams might use to advance themselves from one developmental stage to another.

**VARIATION**   Provide players with pencils and copies of the Team Stages Puzzle. Divide them into four groups based on the four development stages (i.e., forming, storming, norming, and performing). As groups, have them focus on the box containing their assigned developmental stage. Give them two minutes to circle behavior examples in their assigned box that are typical of that stage. Go over the correct answers. Declare teams circling all correct answers winners.

**FOR MORE**
**INFORMATION**   Orsburn, J., Moran, L., Musselwhite, E., & Zenger, J. (1990). *Self-directed work teams.* Chicago, IL: Business One Irwin.

Answers: Forming, cross out 2 & 5; Storming, cross out 1 & 4; Norming, cross out 4 & 5; Performing, cross out 3.

# Team Stages Puzzle

**Directions:** The boxes below are labeled according to the developmental stages through which self-directing work teams commonly pass. Each box contains examples of team members' behaviors that are typical during one of the four stages. Carefully read the behaviors in the respective boxes. Cross out (i.e., draw a line through) the behaviors that do not belong in the box. Do not cross out more than a total of seven behaviors.

---

### FORMING

1. Jane has doubts about the team, but thinks it's worth a try.
2. Brian wishes he knew what part he plays on the team.
3. Fred wants to be part of a cohesive group.
4. Many of the team members complain about the problems of coming together.
5. The team covers for Carol's less than stellar work performance.

---

### STORMING

1. As everyone gets to know each other better, Jane sees a bonding pattern.
2. Jim makes snide comments about Fred's "mothering" attitude.
3. Barbara constantly tries to out perform other team members.
4. Barbara feels good about sharing her ideas with the team.
5. John worries about which things he's responsible for and which things require teamwork.

---

### NORMING

1. The team members look to Jane, as the leader, to supply answers to all problems.
2. Brian is amazed at how well Jim and Fred are getting along.
3. John feels that mutual respect is responsible for the team's pleasant harmony.
4. Barbara is keeping an eye on Brian's and Carol's actions.
5. The team members back Jane in a disagreement with the division supervisor.

---

### PERFORMING

1. Jane secures all the information necessary for the team to get the job done.
2. Fred feels much more self-assured in his work as a team member.
3. John fears that being a team member will stifle his creative genius.
4. The team strives to win more recognition than other teams in the division.
5. John is astounded at how innovative the team is.